Winning the
Rat Race
at Work

Winning the Rat Race at Work

Peter R. Garber

First Edition

Multi-Media 📣
P u b l i c a t i o n s   I n c.
Lakefield, Ontario

Winning the Rat Race at Work
by Peter R. Garber

Acquisitions Editor: Kevin Aguanno
Copy Editor: Josette Coppola
Typesetting: Tak Keung Sin
Cover Design: Cheung Hoi and Massive Brain

Published by:
Multi-Media Publications Inc.
R.R. #4B, Lakefield, Ontario, Canada, K0L 2H0

http://www.mmpubs.com/

ISBN (Paperback):   1-895186-68-4
ISBN (Adobe PDF eBook):   1-895186-69-2
ISBN (Microsoft LIT eBook):   1-895186-70-6
ISBN (Mobipocket PRC eBook):   1-895186-72-2
ISBN (Palm PDB eBook):   1-895186-71-4

Published in Canada. Printed in both U.S.A and the United Kingdom.

Library and Archives Canada Cataloguing in Publication

Garber, Peter R
    Winning the rat race at work / Peter R. Garber. -- 1st ed.

Also available in electronic format.
ISBN 1-895186-68-4

1. Success in business. 2. Career development. I. Title.

HF5381.G366 2006   650.1   C2006-901957-6

Table of Contents

Acknowledgments

There are a number of people that I would like to acknowledge that helped create and write this book Most importantly, I would like to thank my wife Nancy and daughters Lauren and Erin who have been part of my own "Rat Race at Work" for most or all of my thirty-year professional career. This is a race that doesn't always end at the end of the workday or at the company gate but usually continues at home and into family time. My family has shared in both my successes and failures over the years and has provided unconditional support and encouragement along the way. In their eyes, I was always right and the forces that worked against me were never of my doing or fault. This is the kind of support that allows you to *lace up your sneakers* and get back in the race again the next workday.

Getting a book published with the name "rat" in the title is not always easy. I would like to thank Kevin Aguanno, Editor at Mult-Media Publications Inc. for keeping an open mind about this slightly different approach to writing a career oriented book. Also many thanks to Josette Coppola, Copy Editor for the book for making the rat race analogy work so effectively.

Finally, I would like to acknowledge everyone who has ever felt that going to work each day is like being part of a rat race. Take comfort that you are not alone but joined by legions of others all just trying to finish the race and hoping to reach at least some of their career and personal goals along the way.

Good luck in the race.

CHAPTER ONE

Welcome to the Rat Race

There is no question that life is getting more stressful at work for everyone in today's increasingly complex world. The pressures to succeed at work are growing to unprecedented proportions for employees at all levels of organizations. Budgets are getting tighter as more and more is being expected from less and less capital. Yesterday's accomplishments are becoming today's performance standards. Careers are put on the line every day as if they were poker chips in a high stakes gamble. The stresses that people must deal with at work are greater today than perhaps ever before. The Rat Race was never this fast in the past.

The problem, of course, is that this is not a game or a sporting event for the spectator's entertainment. This is serious business. At stake in this race are people's careers, lives and futures. There is no doubt that there is a great deal on the line in this race that is going on each and every day you step out the door to go to work.

Winning the Rat Race at Work was written to help you deal with these growing stresses that you must face on the job. It provides guidance and advice for being successful in the increasingly competitive working environment that you find yourself in today. *Winning the Rat Race at Work* is unique in that it will help you as the reader develop your own strategies for success at work. This book can be used for any number of situations that you might find yourself in during your career, including job searches, career development and advancement, career changes or simply finding new challenges in your current job, even if you have been in the same position for a long time.

Like it or not, you are in this race for the duration of your career. However, winning in this race may be defined in any number of ways, and you might even define it differently than your coworkers. This is perfectly fine. An important step to winning this race is establishing your own criteria for success. As you read this book, you will begin to understand that you are in control of more of these factors for success than you might presently realize. The final chapters will offer you the opportunity to exercise this power more by helping you identify your own specific success goals and define them in ways most meaningful to you.

12

Winning the Rat Race at Work will help you discover the best means of managing your unique factors for success so that you can determine your own destiny in your career.

Recognizing this power will help you identify your unique factors for success and discover how to manage them to better determine your own destiny in your career. This is truly a very worthy objective to strive to achieve.

The Race Begins

So, welcome to the Rat Race. This is truly an equal opportunity race. Work is a daily grind to some degree for virtually everyone who has a job. Or at least this is how many, if not most, people who go to work each day feel about their jobs. It doesn't matter if you are the CEO or just a beginner in your career. You are going to be in this race for the duration. The quicker you understand and accept this fact, the better the race will go for you.

The popular analogy that compares going to work with a rat race is developed throughout this book to provide a slightly different perspective on the concept of trying to get ahead at work. This book will help you to see at least some humor in your current work situation, no matter how frustrating or miserable things might seem to be at the present time. Understanding how to deal with the Rat Race at Work will teach you to cope more effectively with even the most difficult situations you must face on the job.

You may be thinking, "I am not a rat nor am I in any race with anyone at work." Granted, you are certainly not a rat, but you may feel like one at times as a result of the daily grind that everyone experiences to some degree as part of his or her job. However, there is no denying that the world of work is becoming more competitive every day. There are but a finite number of really good jobs available in any organization and everyone is constantly looking to improve his or her position at work and in life. If you don't think that you are in a race at work, you may quickly find that you are going to be left behind the rest of the pack.

The health of the economy can have a dramatic effect on not only the availability of jobs in the market but also the work life of those already employed. Job survival skills are important to learn regardless of where you may currently find yourself in the feast or famine cycles of business success. Limited jobs in the market mean that those who are employed may simply have to live with the problems they face in their current positions, at least until other options become available. Even a bad work situation is better than not having a job at all. Conversely, even during good economic times employees may still be pressured to meet the customer demands that the current situation has created. There is really no escape. The Rat Race at Work is going to exist no matter what the situation. You might as well accept the fact that you are in this race, like it or not. But the good news is that you are not alone. Everyone is on the same treadmill, one way or another, with you. So lace up your sneakers and let's begin creating a winning strategy for being successful in this race.

Caught in a Trap

It is not uncommon for people to feel trapped in their jobs. People need to work to survive and support themselves and their families. It can seem like a vicious cycle. The more frustrated you get by things at work, the more this can negatively influence your performance, which can then affect your future prospects on the job. You feel like a rat trapped on one of those tread wheels where you just keep expending more and more energy without ever getting anywhere.

In desperation, you begin looking for ways to get out of your current work situation. Everywhere you turn, you find another obstacle preventing your escape. You begin to realize that you feel like a rat in a maze, not knowing where to turn to get out. The walls seem to get higher and higher, the escape passages more and more elusive. You sense that you have already attempted the same solutions that you are currently trying to employ, with as little success in the past as you are having now. The harder you try, the more frustrated and exhausted you find yourself, with little or nothing to show for your efforts. To make matters worse, it seems that the others in the race are having no problems at all in finding their way through the maze at work. They constantly seem to be able to get the "cheese" without effort or frustration. You wonder what it is that they know, but you don't, that is allowing them to get ahead in the race while you get left behind.

If this is the way you feel about your current career or job situation, be assured that you are not alone. You are joined by literally millions of other people who also share in your frustration about their current jobs and prospects for the future. *Winning the Rat Race at Work* will help you find your way out of the maze and start moving in the direction of your ultimate career goals. It will help you use your energy in more productive and less counterproductive ways to move yourself forward in your career. Learning to deal more effectively with the Rat Race can save you considerable frustration and anxiety. This can help make your life better in any number of ways.

Below is a story about a young man who was definitely feeling like a rat in a maze as a result of his situation at work. This affected not only his career but his personal life as well. As you read this story, think about how your own work situation may be similar and how it may be affecting your life.

Case Study

Fred Thompson had been with the company for six years. It was actually his third job after he graduated from college with a degree in Finance a little over a decade ago. Disappointing him the most about the job was the recollection that when he started working for the company he had thought he was finally where he needed to be to get his career moving forward. He wanted to become the Chief Financial Officer for a progressive company that would recognize his considerable talents and help him develop his potential as a financial manager. He realized that he had a great deal to learn but was willing to work hard and pay whatever price would be required to be successful in his career. As long as he felt that he was moving forward, he was satisfied with his career path. Unfortunately,

Fred no longer felt that he was moving ahead in his career. Recent organizational changes had put him in what he perceived to be a dead-end role in the organization. However, at least for the moment, he didn't feel there was much he could do about his situation. He had a young family to support and couldn't afford to be out of work. Regardless of how frustrated he was about his job and career, the bills at home kept piling up and his debts kept growing.

Simply switching companies again didn't seem like a good idea either. He had already tried that twice before in his career and had only found himself in similar situations. He was beginning to question his own abilities and potential. What if he just didn't have what it took to move ahead in an organization like the company he worked for? Obviously he was doing something wrong, but he didn't understand what it might be. The more he thought about his current dilemma, the more frustrated he got. In a vicious cycle, these feelings began to exert a negative effect on both his home life and his job performance. His relationship with his wife began to suffer and there was increasing tension at home proportionate to the problems he was experiencing at work. Fred was grateful for the support and patience of his wife, believing that without this he wouldn't be able to survive these tumultuous times. To make matters worse, he was still under a great deal of pressure at work to produce despite these grim prospects for career advancement in the foreseeable future. His boss kept piling more and more work on his desk while the only solace offered was a reminder that he was just lucky to still have a job during these difficult times for business today.

17

Although relieved not to be on the unemployment lines, somehow Fred didn't feel very lucky these days when it came to his career. However, he was afraid to complain too much about his current plight for fear of losing his job, considering all the reductions that were currently occurring in not only his organization but also other companies. Fred felt truly trapped like a rat in a cage with no prospects for getting out very soon, if ever.

And so the Rat Race goes. Fred's story may be similar to yours or perhaps you can relate to just parts of it. Regardless, everyone feels some measure of the Rat Race at Work every day. Learning to cope more effectively with these situations can be one of the most valuable skills that you can acquire in your career. The old adage, "If you can't beat 'em, join 'em" might be most applicable when it comes to the Rat Race at Work. The more you try to deny that you are in this race or try to sit on the sidelines, the worse your situation at work will likely become. So put on those running shoes and get in the race. Like it or not, you're in this race for the rest of your working life and career.

Perspectives

Sometimes it can be easy to lose perspective on a problem.
Problems can easily seem to become bigger than life. The
proportion of the problem can seem to be enormous, and the
lines between your working life and your personal life can easily
become blurred. Your self-esteem, ego, and sense of security
can quickly seem threatened by a situation at work. There is no
doubt that each of these personal factors in your life is on the
line every day you go to work. But keeping the proper
perspective on problems at work is important in gaining back
control of a bad work situation. Keep in mind that there are
distinctions between your personal self and your professional
or working self and that there are times when they must
intertwine and times when they must be kept apart.

Roles

To keep these delineations clear, it is helpful to visualize your
roles in each of these important aspects of your life. The figure
on the next page is an illustration of the different roles you play
in your life.

We actually have three major roles we play in our lives:
Self, Relationships and *Job. Self* refers to the things that we do
for ourselves that keep us happy and functioning. This might
include our hobbies, interests, habits, etc. *Relationships* refers
to our dealings with others. These relationships include our
families, friends, colleagues and others that we come in contact
with on a regular basis. *Job* in this model refers to that part of
our lives that we dedicate to our careers. Each is critically

Job
Relationships
Self

important to one's happiness and success in life. Of course, the degree of importance that each person places on each of these three roles is an individualized matter. Often the balance between these three roles may seem threatened. One of these roles may become dominant over the others. An individual may focus too much of his or her time and energy on one of these roles at the expense of the others. When this happens, the natural balance in our lives begins to suffer. Consequences emerge as a result. For some people, these consequences may be acceptable and believed to be a reasonable cost for the potential benefits to be achieved. However, the true consequences of these roles being out of balance may not be realized immediately. It may take many years before they completely manifest themselves. People often look back on their lives and realize (albeit too late) that they have miscalculated their priorities in life. No matter what rewards may have been achieved in one of these roles, they are sometimes totally eclipsed by failures due to lack of attention in the others.

Pressures to be successful at work can often upset the balance between these roles. One of the greatest consequences of the Rat Race at Work is that people's *job* roles often seem to take center stage in their lives. When this happens, the *relationships* role suffers, sometimes irreparably. Issues relating to *self* may also suffer and may lead to health problems both physical and mental. As one aspect of a person's life begins to crumble, it often takes the others along in the decline. Fortunately, Fred Thompson in the case described above had a supportive spouse to help keep his relationships with others from becoming a consequence of the problems he was experiencing at work. Unfortunately, this is not always the case in every situation.

Roles Out of Balance

Too often in today's society, people feel "the end justifies the means" when it comes to dedicating extensive amounts of time to their careers, time taken away from family and/or friends. This often leads to a breakdown in one or more of these life roles. The end result is a life grossly out of balance in terms of nurturing the three major roles we play in life in appropriate proportions, and this imbalance is illustrated in the figure on the next page.

Although often the culprit, the job is not always what dominates the other aspects of a person's life. There are situations in which either the *self* or the *relationships* role takes

center stage in a person's life. This may be for justifiable
reasons such as an illness or some other life crisis that
necessitates that personal issues take precedence over one's
career. In any case, the natural balance of these roles is
disturbed and life cannot return to normal until this
equilibrium is reestablished. However, it is important both to
understand and to accept the fact that these imbalances will
occur in life. Part of dealing effectively with a significant
personal problem is to allow these role imbalances to exist
during the troubling times. Employers typically understand
that these imbalances occur in the lives of their employees and
provide disability programs as part of their overall benefits to
help out in these situations. There are a number of federal and

state employment laws, such as the Family and Medical Leave Act or the Americans with Disabilities Act, that also provide benefits and protections for employees who are experiencing problems requiring additional help to adjust or adapt to their current situation.

How long these roles are out of balance will depend on each particular situation as well as the individual. Some people have a need to return to work as quickly as possible following an illness or personal crisis. Others need more time to make the adjustment. Each individual must determine just how long he or she can afford to have these roles out of balance and what support he or she needs during these transition periods. It is important to remember that each of these roles must be nurtured and maintained. Focusing on any one of these roles to an extreme can threaten the others. True success in life is best achieved by maintaining a healthy balance between these important roles we play in life. Keeping the Rat Race at Work from dominating your other roles in life should be one of your most important goals.

The following self-assessment is designed to help you better understand how you may currently be balancing these three roles in your life. Please take a few moments to complete this brief survey. A scoring key is provided below it so that you may interpret the results after you have finished.

Role Self-Assessment

Circle the answer to each of the following questions that best describes how you would feel or respond in each of the scenarios presented in this self-assessment. Remember, there are no absolute right or wrong answers to this assessment tool. Answer these questions according to your current behaviors and priorities rather than how you might want this balance in the future. You will be referring to the results of this survey throughout the rest of this book as you begin to develop more effective balance strategies.

A. Your boss calls you into his/her office late Friday afternoon and tells you that a big project you have been working on needs to be completed a week ahead of the original schedule. You had thought that you would be able to finish the report sometime next week, but now it is due on the following Monday. You had planned to spend the weekend with your family as you have been spending so much time away from them lately because of this project. What would you do?

1. Cancel your personal plans and spend the entire weekend in the office.

2. Tell your family that you need to spend time finishing the project over the weekend because of the change in the completion date. Spend as much time with them as you can over the weekend and still complete the project.

3. Schedule time over the weekend to meet as many of the commitments you made to your job, family and yourself as you can, including working on your hobby.

B. A job opens up that would be a big promotion for you. You would love to have the job but you know that it will involve considerably more hours of work than is normal for you. Select the answer below that best describes how you would deal with this situation:

1. Tell your boss that you want the job and that you would be willing to put in as many hours as needed to be successful.

2. Discuss with your family how the promotion would affect them and decide together whether you should accept the promotion or not.

3. Think about how the required commitment to the new job would affect your life and outside interests before deciding to take the promotion or not.

C. Something suddenly comes up at work that will require your immediate attention for the next several days. The problem is that you also have a vacation scheduled with your family at the same time. Your employer asks you to stay and deal with the problem and offers to give you another week off at a later date. What would you do?

1. Cancel your vacation and deal with the problem at work.

2. Go on vacation with your family.

3. Stay home and spend part of the time dealing with the work problem and the rest of the week pursuing your own personal interests. Reschedule the family vacation for another time.

D. For which of the following reasons would you be most likely to leave work early?

1. There was a work-related problem at another location that requires your attention.

2. A family member is involved in an activity that you would like to attend.

3. You would like to pursue a personal interest or hobby.

E. Which of the following seminars would you be most interested in attending if given the opportunity?

1. A job skills improvement class that would significantly help you in your career

2. A seminar on building better interpersonal relationships

3. A seminar or lesson that would improve skills or knowledge relating to a hobby of yours

F. If you were threatened with the loss of your job, which of the following actions would you most likely take?

1. Immediately begin working more hours to try to make yourself more valuable to your employer

2. Talk to your family about the situation and develop a plan together about how to deal with this situation

3. Consider this an opportunity to change careers to something that would be more meaningful and rewarding to you

G. You are given the chance to transfer to another position in the company. Although this change would be a promotion and an excellent career opportunity, it would require moving your family to another location. You are told that the company needs your decision as quickly as possible. What would you do?

1. Tell the company that you feel certain that you will accept the position but you need to discuss it with your family that evening.

2. Tell the company that you need to discuss this with your family and that you will let them know your decision in the next few days.

3. Ask more about the career opportunities that this position will offer before you even begin to consider accepting the job or not.

H. How often do you check your work-related voice mail messages or emails in your free time such as during weekends or vacations?

1. Regularly throughout these times regardless of what you may be involved in doing at the moment

2. Only when it doesn't interfere with an activity with family or friends

3. You only check these messages if you are expecting someone to contact you about something of personal interest to you

I.   What would you be most willing to sacrifice in order to be considered for a big promotion in your organization?

1.   Some time away from your family and friends or pursuing your personal interests

2.   Nothing that would take significant amounts of time away from your family over an extended period

3.   Nothing that would significantly interfere with your personal life, interests or activities for a considerable period of time

J.   Which of the following statements best describes your personal philosophy about the purpose of work?

1.   To make the greatest contribution to the organization during your career

2.   To be able to provide for your family

3.   To develop and grow both personally and professionally to reach the highest level you possibly can during your career

K. You have just received a memo from your organization announcing a pay freeze for this year. You have put in many extra hours working on a big project during this past year and you were expecting a big raise as a result of your efforts. How would you react to this situation?

1. Realize that the organization is currently experiencing financial difficulties and support the decision to freeze salaries for the present time

2. Explain to your family why you will not be receiving a raise this year despite all the time you spent away from them during the past year

3. Consider the extra time and effort you put into the project during the past year as a developmental opportunity that will help you in your future career advancement

L. Suppose that a recruiting firm calls you and tells you about a career opportunity with another organization. You might be interested in the job but there are a number of things that must be taken into consideration before you would be willing to consider this opportunity. Which of the following factors would be most important to you in making this decision?

1. The job itself

2. The location of the job

3. The career potential and personal development that the job would offer

Interpreting Your Score

Each of the "1" answers in the assessment were directed towards *job* tendencies in relation to balance in one's life. Similarly, "2" answers were directed towards *relationships* tendencies and "3" answers were directed towards *self* tendencies. Count how many answers you selected that were numbered "1," "2" or "3" and record below:

___ 1. *Job* Answers

___ 2. *Relationships* Answers

___ 3. *Self* Answers

Ideally, you should have an equal balance (a score of 4 for each role) between your roles relating to *job, relationships* and *self.* Each role supports the other two. Many problems can be created in one's life when one or more of these roles get out of balance, particularly if it is at the expense of the others. Based on the results of this brief self-assessment, think about how you may currently be balancing these three roles.

Chapter Summary

There is no question that work is becoming more and more of a challenge for most people every day. It can seem like an intense competition in which not everyone can even complete the contest, much less end up in the winner's circle. However, you have no choice but to stay in this race for the duration of your working career. You may have no control over many of the factors that create whatever situation you must deal with at work each day in the Rat Race at Work. However, you do have control over how you react to the situation. Your values, you goals and even your ideals are still your own. These can be the most important factors in determining the satisfaction you have concerning your job and perhaps your overall happiness in life. The value you place on the roles you play in your life can be the most significant determinants in Winning the Rat Race at Work. The criteria for winning this race should be your own, not something imposed on you or dictated to you by anyone else. This book will help you keep these important factors in perspective as you move towards the finish line in your career. *Winning the Rat Race at Work* will help you achieve some of your own personal victories along the way and maintain balance in the roles you play in life.

CHAPTER TWO

The Rat Race Maze

Your situation at work can make you feel like you are truly caught in a maze, not knowing which way to turn. If you go down the wrong path, it can take you farther from your career expectations and goals. Other directions can truly become career dead ends. You can easily begin to feel like there is no good way out of the predicament that you find yourself in today. How do you know which way to turn?

If you have ever played a game in which you had to find your way out of a maze, the first lesson you should have learned is that you need to keep your wits about you. The worst thing that you can do is to waste a lot of energy randomly trying to find your way out of the maze without some kind of plan or strategy. All you will do is to keep going down the same paths leading you nowhere but getting you more and more lost and farther away from the true direction you really wish to go. The maze is like any other problem you might attempt to solve. There are solutions to every problem, often many different ones to be found.

Your career is very much like a maze in many different ways. There might be any number of paths that you can take to find your way through this career maze. Not everyone will take the same career path. Some of these paths will be created for you. Others need to be explored on your own. Some pathways may appear to be promising in the beginning, only to become dead ends. Until you go down those pathways, you may not truly know which ones will lead you out of the maze and which ones will block your career progress. Regardless, there are many lessons to be learned along this journey. How well you learn these lessons may become a major factor in the success that you experience during your career.

Solving Your Career Maze

There are certain critical factors that you should look for to help you solve your career maze. These factors are like clues to solving the maze. They can become a set of directions to help you reach your ultimate career destination. However, these clues may not always be readily apparent. You often have to search carefully to find them along your career journey. There are no signs along the way telling you in which direction to travel. You may indeed have to look very hard, even create some of these clues for yourself. However, these clues are discoverable. Each clue will help you navigate your way through your career maze, providing direction and guidance along the way. These clues, however, are not foolproof. They can be deceiving and can sometimes lead you in the wrong direction. This may be due to a matter of timing or some other uncontrollable factor that changes the direction you need to travel. Often you need to change your plans or career strategy to adjust to these changes when they appear. Flexibility and the ability to go in different directions depending on the situation are key to solving the career maze. Going through the maze will help you better visualize the obstacles and challenges that you must face in order to be successful at work.

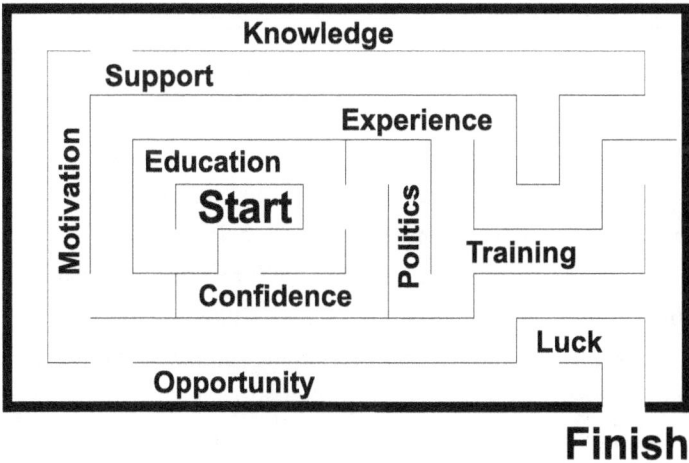

35

Career Maze Factors

The following Career Maze Factors will help you find your way through the maze. Many of these factors will be covered in greater detail later on in this book. They are being introduced as part of the maze to illustrate how each one interrelates with the others, creating even greater challenges for you to face in your career. Remember that there can be many different directions that you might take to get to your ultimate career destination and more than one solution to every problem.

Education

Education is becoming more and more of a core requirement in many occupations. Without the proper educational credentials, you may have much less chance of ever working your way through this career maze. Some occupations require specific degrees without which you cannot qualify to work in the field. To continue trying to pursue a particular career without the required degree may only cause you to become farther and farther off course in the maze. In other fields of work, education becomes a foundation for the understanding that you must have in order to be successful. Education may also serve as the differential in qualifying candidates for entry into a career. Scholastic accomplishment is often used in selection decisions concerning which candidate to hire out of a pack of many qualified applicants. Although this may not always serve as an accurate predictor of future success, it still is one of the few truly objective selection criteria available for employers to utilize to hire the candidate most likely to be successful on the job.

One fact that many people forget is that education should be a lifelong endeavor. It doesn't have to end at a certain age or point in your life. Many employers provide generous education assistance programs for those employees willing to take on the challenge of working and going back to school at the same time, along with balancing family commitments. If you are able to meet these challenges, there may be different career directions available that otherwise would have been inaccessible.

Education is one of the best advantages that one can have when beginning a career journey. However, it is not the only factor that is important to solving the career maze. The right education may get you off to a great start and even open up doors that otherwise would have been closed. But you shouldn't depend on education alone to make you successful. There are a number of other factors that also must be considered or you can become hopelessly lost in the career maze.

Training

There are many forms of job training that occur during a person's career. Actually, training begins the very first day you start any job. This training may be part of a structured, formal program designed by the organization, or it may be something that just happens as a result of someone's being on the job day after day. Let's examine these two types of training experiences one may receive on the job and the advantages and disadvantages of each:

Formal Training -Typically we think of formal job training as something that the organization develops to help teach its employees how to do their jobs. This training may involve actual classroom-type experiences explicitly designed to provide technical and job-specific knowledge to the employee. Often this knowledge is unique to the organization and its operations. Formal training may also be more generic to the organization such as programs designed to make everyone more aware of the need for improved quality or greater diversity at work. The primary advantage of this type of training is that it ensures that everyone gains this knowledge and understanding. It also provides the benefit that everyone in the organization goes through the learning experience together and at the same time. This can heighten the learning experience and create a greater awareness and application of the principles taught in these formal training programs. Perhaps the only potential downside of this type of training is the cost. Training can be very expensive to an organization in direct costs such as training materials, licenses, consultants, seminar fees, travel expenses, etc. It also involves indirect costs to the organization in terms of the productivity lost while employees are attending these programs.

Informal Training - There are many ways in which informal training can be provided to employees. This may be in the form of structured learning experiences that only real-life, on-the-job training can provide. This works best when there are specific learning objectives established for the incumbents in the job to experience. However, often this type of training experience is unstructured and random. It is assumed that sooner or later the trainee will experience everything he or she will need during this indoctrination period for future success on the job. This may or may not occur. The major problem with on-the-job training is that often you are given the *test* before you have been given the opportunity to take the *course*. Informal training usually works best when it is combined with some form of formal or structured training program that monitors on-the-job learning experiences to ensure that an employee is ready to handle the challenges of the job. Although informal training programs are often perceived as more economical, this may not ultimately prove to be true. Lack of proper training can cost the organization significant amounts of capital in terms of lost productivity, downtime, turnover, and unhappy customers.

The reason why many people may feel trapped at work is that they haven't been given the proper training to be able to competently perform their jobs. Not receiving the proper training is like entering a race and being physically held back at the starting line. Lack of training can put you in a distinctly unfair disadvantage over the rest of the pack in the race. Ultimately, you need to be in charge of your own training and development. If you are not satisfied with the training you have received on your job, you should discuss this situation with your boss or supervisor. Come prepared with a practical plan that could help develop your job knowledge and skills. Think of ways in which you could benefit from both formal and informal training experiences. The right training experiences can help you get past the obstacles that may currently be standing in the way of your career goals.

Experience

Experience is a form of informal training, but it also has other attributes as well. Experience itself is life's greatest teacher. This is different than informal training in that experience helps you grow and develop in ways that can't be taught. Experience doesn't merely teach you how to perform your job; it also defines who you are as a person and an employee. In many ways, you are a product of every experience that you have encountered during your lifetime. The problem is that we often don't take advantage of our experiences and the lessons that they have provided. We constantly find ourselves making the same mistakes over and over again in our lives. Life is actually a series of lessons we keep learning and relearning. In order to compete in the Rat Race at Work, you need to be able to recycle some of these lessons instead of learning them over and over again. When faced with a problem or challenge at work, you need to stop and reflect on similar problems and solutions that you have previously experienced. Think about how well the potential solutions, as applied to those past situations, worked. It is said that insanity is trying to do the same things over and over again and expecting different outcomes than in the past. No matter how good a solution may sound, if it hasn't been successful in the past there may be no basis to believe that there will be any different results in the future.

Use your experiences both on the job and in life to help you navigate your way through the maze at work. There is a great deal of knowledge stored in your past experiences that could be better applied to solving future problems.

Politics

Chapter Four of this book is dedicated to this factor and the role that internal politics plays in your career. There is no question that organizational politics plays an important and often significant role in your success during your career. To ignore politics at work is a big mistake, one that might hopelessly trap you in an unhappy career. You may not be able to do very much about the politics in your organization, but you do at least need to respect the influence that politics may have on your career. However, there are ways in which you can keep yourself from becoming trapped in your career because of these politics. There are even ways in which you can use these politics to help move you forward in your career. As you read Chapter Four, think about this maze and what you can do to prevent organizational politics from becoming an obstacle and possibly even derive benefit from it during your career.

Knowledge

There really is no substitute for good old-fashioned knowledge when it comes to being successful on the job. Knowledge is the great equalizer. Knowledge doesn't play favorites or hold prejudices. Either you are knowledgeable about your job or field of supposed expertise or you are not. Unfortunately, there are always pretenders of knowledge in every job. These people pose one of the greatest threats to the organization. In the wrong roles, they can be very dangerous because others look to them for advice but can't depend on its accuracy. The problem is that knowledge is not always evenly distributed. If there isn't a subject matter expert available to make certain decisions or answer important questions, the organization could be in big trouble.

However, this is perhaps one of the greatest fallacies of the maze. Knowledge pretenders can slip through the maze as if they were the real things. But don't despair; real knowledge is also required in order to navigate successfully through the maze in the long run. With any luck, these pretenders will eventually be discovered. Having knowledge about your job and really knowing what you are doing will give you a great advantage in the challenges that lie ahead in the Rat Race a Work.

Support

Having the support you need to perform your job effectively can be one of the greatest benefits you can have during your career. Without the proper support, your job can seem virtually impossible to perform. Support can come in many different forms and ways. Support might be the backing of key people in your organization (including your boss) concerning the initiatives that you need to undertake as part of your job. Nothing is more frustrating than to be told to do something but not be given the resources necessary to get the job done. Unfortunately, this is a common scenario too frequently played out during many employees' careers. With the right support, seemingly impossible tasks can be accomplished. It is amazing what can get done in an organization when the right people are committed to the task or goal.

Support may at first seem like one of those factors that are not within your control. However, this may not necessarily be true. Ask yourself this question: "Have I really tried to get the support of those in my organization that play a key role in accomplishing the task or goal?" If you have not, you could be stalling your progress in navigating the maze when the right support could keep you moving ahead in your career.

Motivation

Winning the Rat Race at Work, like genius, is as much about perspiration as it is about anything else. Effort can overcome many obstacles and help you find your way through the maze at work. Motivation to be successful in the race can become the greatest differential between those who are ultimately successful and those who are not. Those who work hardest to reach their aspirations are often the ones to achieve their career goals. If you think that this is going to be an easy race to run, you will be greatly disappointed. What is needed is the desire to succeed and the motivation to do what it takes to reach your goals. Often the winner in any contest is the individual or team that wanted the most to be victorious.

Confidence

Confidence is something that is difficult to define but easy to recognize. Confidence can't be fabricated—it must be genuine. Confidence is a contagious condition and can spill over to other aspects of your life as well. Once confidence is caught, it can last for a long time. This is a good thing. Confidence begets confidence. One success often creates another. People have confidence in those who have confidence in themselves. Confidence helps you keep going even in the face of potential failure. Confidence allows even missteps to be turned into successes. Confidence opens doors that would not be opened otherwise. Confidence can guide you on your way through the maze at work even during the most challenging times.

Remember, you wouldn't have achieved what you have in your life so far if you didn't have the ability to be successful. You need to have confidence in yourself and your capacity to be successful in the future. Think about what made you successful in the past. You are still the same person who created these past successes and you can create future successes as well. All you need is a little confidence and the rest will fall into place.

Opportunity

Opportunity is an essential ingredient for any formula for success. Without opportunity, even the best of efforts can be all for naught. Opportunities must exist for winners to emerge from the rest of the pack. During hard times, the number of opportunities may diminish. However, if you sit and wait for opportunity to knock on your door you may find yourself left behind everyone else in the race. Winners make their own opportunities.

Often you need to try different things to find what might work best for you and give you the greatest chance for success in your career. Being willing to go in different directions during your career can make many new avenues to success possible. This can create opportunities to fail as well as to succeed. Without risk there may be no opportunity to be successful. Every challenge brings new opportunities to succeed. Looking for new opportunities can take you in new directions that can help you move your way through the maze.

Luck

Luck is a factor in just about any successful endeavor. But doesn't it seem that some people were just born lucky? They seem to get all the breaks in their careers. They always seem to be in the right place at the right time, to know the right people, to enjoy the best connections, and to have just what is needed in any situation. How did they get so lucky?

Are these people really lucky or do they do things that always seem to put them in an advantaged position? It is said that you make your own luck in life. Think about what these supposedly lucky people might have done that made them so lucky. Think about how you can make some luck for yourself in your career and even your life.

How Well are You Getting Through Your Career Maze?

Instructions: How well do you feel you are progressing through your career maze? Using the following symbols, circle each Critical Maze Factor you believe best represents your progress in the Rat Race at Work.

⌐ = Career Progress Completely Blocked

⌐ = Some Career Progress but Eventually Blocked

— = Career Progress Moving Forward Unblocked

Education	⌐ ⌐ —
Training	⌐ ⌐ —
Experience	⌐ ⌐ —
Politics	⌐ ⌐ —
Knowledge	⌐ ⌐ —
Support	⌐ ⌐ —
Motivation	⌐ ⌐ —
Confidence	⌐ ⌐ —
Opportunity	⌐ ⌐ —
Luck	⌐ ⌐ —

Maze Factor Scoring

Give yourself a score of 0 for each factor that you rated as a ⌐

Give yourself a score of 10 for each factor you rated as a ⌐

Give yourself a score of 25 for each factor you rated as a —

Total Score _____

If you scored between **0–100**, you may need to find new paths to move forward through the career maze.

If you scored between **100-200**, you have already found many ways to navigate the maze but still have some factors that need to be paid more attention to in the future

If you scored **200-250**, you are already well on your way to Winning the Rat Race at Work.

Applying the Maze Results to Your Career

Review the 5 critical factors for which you scored the **lowest** on the maze. List those factors below:

_____

_____

_____

_____

_____

Now look at the 5 factors for which you scored the **highest**.
List those factors below:

_____

_____

_____

_____

_____

Chapter Summary

As you progress through your career, you will be faced with
many challenges. These challenges present both potential
obstacles and possible opportunities for you along your career
journey. If you expect ever to win the Rat Race at Work, you
must pay attention to these critical factors for success.

As you read the rest of this book, focus particularly on
those topics relating to the factors revealed in your self-
evaluation as needing the most attention. In the following
chapters you will find advice and guidance that can help you
turn these deficiencies into strengths that can help you move
ahead in your career. Be sure also to pay attention to ways that
you can further develop your career strengths so they may
continue guiding your way through your career maze in the
future as well.

CHAPTER THREE

The Rat Race is On

I magine that your career is actually like a horse race similar to the Kentucky Derby, with an announcer calling the action as the pack rounds the turns on the track. It might just sound something like this:

> *And they're off . . . with* New Employees *and* Fresh out of College *challenging the* Veteran Employees *for the really good jobs that exist in the organization. But* Experience *still edges ahead by a nose. On the rail is* Boss's Favorite *followed closely by* Recent Promotion. *In the middle of the pack are* Late Bloomer *and* Highly Motivated. *As they turn into the final stretch, bringing up the rear is* Disenchanted *and* Bad Work Attitude.

And so the race begins and never really ends for anyone who has to work for a living. No matter if you are just beginning your career or approaching retirement, you are in the race for the duration of your working days. The problem is that sometimes people have a tendency to sit out this race and watch others pass them by. This is something that doesn't have to happen. It is never too soon or too late to get back in the race. Careers can be rejuvenated at any time. Just like the veteran actor who finally wins that Academy Award that has eluded him or her for so many years, success can come at any time and at any age or stage of a career. Even those who are approaching retirement in the foreseeable future can still benefit from this advice.

The key is getting back in the race. You will never become competitive if you simply sit in the bleachers and watch everyone else run the race. You need to lace up your running shoes and get down on the track. However, this can be a difficult and even frightening task for many who may have been on the sidelines for a long time. This chapter deals with not only getting started in the race but also staying motivated throughout your entire career.

Stages of a Career

A typical career goes through a series of stages throughout the working life of an individual. Each stage has different characteristics and needs to be fulfilled. Each stage represents transitional steps to the next stage. It is possible to skip a stage, but when this happens the needs of the excluded stage may manifest themselves in some way in later stages. Understanding these stages can help you assess where you are in your career progression and navigate your way in the Rat Race at Work. The 5 stages of a career are entry, development, progression, optimization, and plateau.

Entry

The entry stage of a career obviously begins with Day One on the job and typically continues for at least a year or two, depending on the job. This is a learning period, not only technically but organizationally as well. During this stage of a career, the individual is learning how to work his or her way through the organizational maze.

Development

This is the stage of a career where most job skills are learned, maybe even mastered. It is during this time in a career when the true abilities of an employee really begin to emerge. This is perhaps the most important stage of a person's career. If this development stage is not allowed to progress properly, critical learning opportunities may be lost forever. The person may be able to continue being promoted in his or her career but will always be lacking in knowledge and expertise. The development stage of a career typically lasts no longer than 3 years.

Progression

Progression is the stage when you should really begin to move ahead during your career. By this stage you have gained the skills and competencies necessary for future advancement in your career. During years 5 to 10 at this stage in a career, an employee has the potential to position himself or herself higher up in the organization. Career decisions and career development can be most important at this stage, creating future opportunities. The competition may become most intense at this stage of careers as others are also setting aggressive career goals for the future.

Optimization

The Optimization stage of a career typically begins anytime after 10 years but can begin earlier. This is when people really get their stride during their careers. By this point you have the training, experience and perspective to truly reach your greatest potential and make the greatest contribution. Often the degree of optimization that is achieved in a career is dependent on the opportunities that are available during this time period. This is when the greatest challenges in a career can best be met and goals realized.

Plateau

Plateaus often occur during the final stage or stages of a career. When a career hits a plateau it doesn't necessarily mean that a person's skills have declined but rather that there may be no more *mountains* to climb. In other words, the individual has accomplished everything he or she can during the career. When one begins to see the endpoint of his or her career, different values begin to gain dominance. As people approach retirement eligibility, they begin to think about entering the next stage of their lives. Their careers may no longer be the

main source of resources in their lives. Career advancement
may no longer seem to be a reasonable expectation and the
person begins to enter more of a maintenance rather than a
development mode. However, there are exceptions when
individuals continue to perform at an optimum level right up
to the dates of their retirements. How the individual is
perceived and the type of assignments he or she receives during
this stage of a career can be a determining motivational factor.

Each of these stages follows the learning curve typically
experienced during a career. This learning curve is shown
below with each of these stages identified as to when they
usually occur during a career.

These 5 stages of a career are shown on the graph
below:

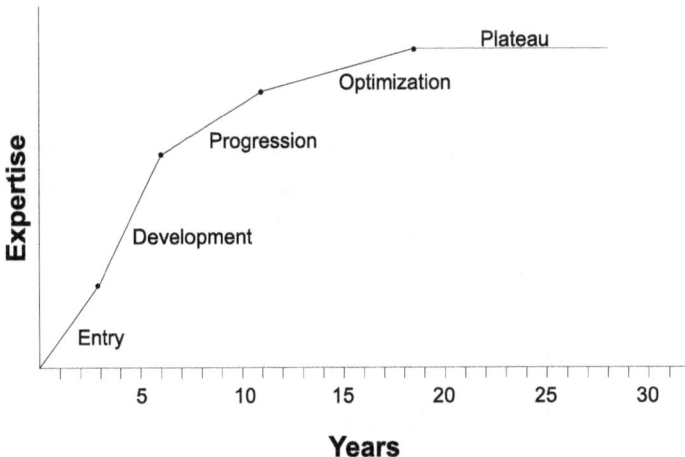

What stage of your career are you in now? On the
above graph, mark the stage of your career you are in today.

With this improved vision of where you currently are in your career, how can you optimize the remaining stages of your career to help you achieve your career goals?

Getting Off to a Good Start

In any race or competition, getting off to a good start is critically important to your success and how well you finish in the end. Getting off to a good start in your career can be equally important. Like any competitor, from the moment you start the contest you need to set goals about your position as you cross the finish line at the end of the race. How you begin the race can have a huge impact on how you finish. This can be a significant determinant in where you end up in the pack. Making good decisions early on in your career can make a big difference in positioning you for greater opportunities later on in your career. Actually, retirement planning should begin on the first day and be part of everything you do during your career, even though that may be about the last thing on your mind when you start out in the world of work. However, making good career decisions is important at any time during your career. Even the best decisions made early in one's career can be completely negated by poorer decisions later on in the race to the finish line called retirement.

Career Roads

In his poem "The Road Not Taken," the poet Robert Frost ponders the path he did not choose and where it might have led. We travel along many roads on our way to our career destinations. Some of these roads we choose and some are

The Road Not Taken

by Robert Frost (1916)

Two roads diverged in a yellow wood,
And sorry I could not travel both
And be one traveler, long I stood
And looked down one as far as I could
To where it bent in the undergrowth;

Then took the other, as just as fair,
And having perhaps the better claim,
Because it was grassy and wanted wear;
Though as for that the passing there
Had worn them really about the same,

And both that morning equally lay
In leaves no step had trodden black.
Oh, I kept the first for another day!
Yet knowing how way leads on to way,
I doubted if I should ever come back.

I shall be telling this with a sigh
Somewhere ages and ages hence:
Two roads diverged in a wood, and I—
I took the one less traveled by,
And that has made all the difference.

Reprinted from Frost, Robert. *Mountain Interval.* New York: Henry Holt and Company, 1920. Used with permission.

chosen for us. Each plays an important part in our lives. Often, it is helpful to see where these roads have already taken us. Knowing where we have been can help guide us to where we are going. We can see which roads led toward our goals and which did not. An old proverb says, "Even the longest journey begins with the first step." We actually begin preparing for our eventual careers at very young ages. Our performance in school and in other activities may lead us towards or away from certain career possibilities.

The Roads We Choose

Looking back on past decisions made, you will never really know where some of those *roads not taken* may have led. All you can do is to look forward and make the best decisions at the time based on the information available to you. Sometimes the biggest challenges are when we come to those proverbial forks in the road. The baseball great Yogi Berra offers some advice for this dilemma: "If you come to a fork in the road— take it." If only it were that simple, Yogi. Unfortunately, we do have to make difficult career decisions in our lives. Sometimes we have to live with these decisions for many years, maybe even an entire career. The roads that you take will have a significant influence on the rest of your life. It has been said that true success is achieved by enjoying what you do for a living and getting paid for it at the same time. If you are just beginning your career journey or perhaps are contemplating a change, choose your employer carefully; your career and perhaps your happiness may depend on it.

Conflicting Maps

The problem is that you can't simply pull into a rest stop along these career roads and pick up a map that will give you precise information concerning where you currently are in your journey and where you need to go to reach your ultimate destination. Compounding the problem is that the few tools that you might have available to guide you along the way may give you conflicting information. One source may guide you in one direction and another in a different way. Imagine what it would be like if you purchased a standard road map containing conflicting information. Without a crystal ball, how can one ever expect to know exactly which career roads to take? The answer is that there aren't any guarantees about success. Make the best decisions you can and remember that there will be many other decision points during your career that will be equally important to your ultimate success during your journey.

Beginning Your Career Journey

Mapping out a plan can help you make better career decisions along your journey. It can provide you with a vision of what your journey may be like in the future, as seen from the information available to you at the present time. Factors that should be considered in this career mapping exercise include your career expectations and aspirations, the career opportunities that are available and the obstacles that you may encounter along the way. Again, unlike a traditional road map, this map is one that is dynamic. It will by necessity need to change according to the environment in which it exists. Career opportunities expand and contract, often following the business cycle. The success of the company or organization in which one is employed also plays a big part in the career advancement opportunities that may or may not exist for the individual.

Destinations

Another old proverb says, "If you don't know where you are going, almost any road can take you there." That is like beginning a journey without a destination or a road map; you are likely to end up driving around in circles and never getting anywhere. Career goals may not always lead you to your destination, but they help to guide your choices and decisions and improve your chances of ending up somewhere you want to be.

In the example that follows, a Career Map is shown of an individual moving from an entry level Sales Trainee position to a Marketing Manager position. You can see the progression of jobs that lead to the Marking Manager position. Notice the scale of time: it will take about ten years to reach this point in the person's career. Of course, a lot of things could happen during those years and the person will have to make some career decisions along the way. The individual will also need guidance on his journey and may even have to ask for directions, something that certain people may have difficulty doing.

Sales Trainee

Marketing Representative

Sales Representative

Marketing Manager

Time Line (years)   5   10

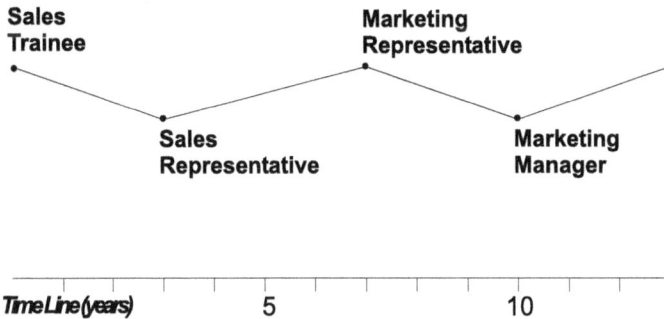

What Are Your Destinations?

Reflect back on your own career for a few moments. What would your Career Map look like at this point in your journey? Answer the following questions to help you better visualize where you began, where you are today and where you are heading in your career.

Think about how your journey began. Did you make a conscious choice regarding your career?

What led you to this choice?

61

Would you make that choice today? Why or why not?

State, in a few sentences, what your career goal is now.

Directions

Each choice we make can have far-reaching consequences. In
the next illustrated example, the salesperson might decide in
the fifth year of his or her career to move into the advertising
department. You can see what the possible outcome might have
been from this key career decision. Sometimes the best
directions are not obvious and career decisions are not easy to
make. You may even have to stop along the way and ask for
directions (something very difficult to do for many people,
especially men!). Some careers have many roads to choose from
and others have relatively few. In each case, it is important to
attempt to know the direction in which each road leads. When
making career decisions, it can be helpful to actually draw a
map of where you believe each road will take you. The better
you can visualize in what directions you may be heading in the
future, the more successful you will be in the Rat Race at Work.

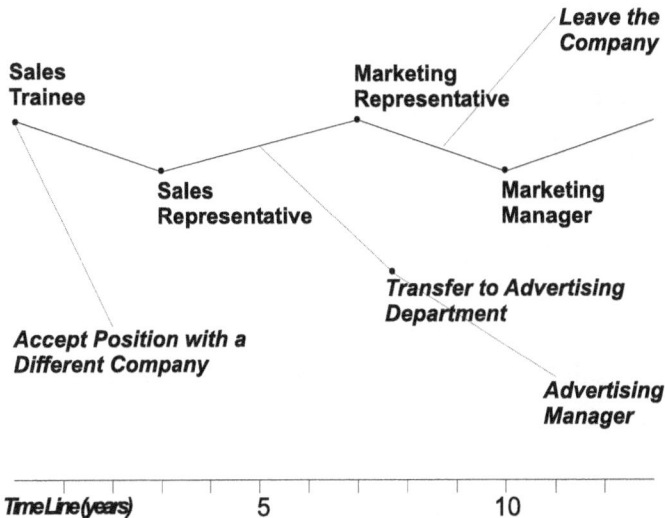

Sales Trainee

Sales Representative

Marketing Representative

Leave the Company

Marketing Manager

Transfer to Advertising Department

Accept Position with a Different Company

Advertising Manager

TimeLine(years)   5   10

63

What Are Your Directions?

Next, think about the direction your own career has taken and answer the following questions:

Do you feel that you have exercised much choice in the direction in which your career has gone?

How has taking or changing a direction affected your expected career path?

How different might your career have been today had you gone down some of the "roads not taken"?

Are you headed in the right direction that is likely to lead to your stated career goals?

If not, how can you get back on track to be headed in the direction of your career goals?

How do you typically make such decisions?

Do you think that is the best way for you to make such decisions?

Tolls

Like any road, the career road often includes tolls that must be
paid. A toll may be simply completing a training program or it
may involve moving to a different city, state or even country.
Some career roads require changing jobs or gaining experience
in several different organizations or earning an advanced
degree. Other tolls include working long hours, and this, like
relocation, can have a detrimental effect on family
relationships. As one's career progresses, the tolls may seem to
be more "expensive," as is shown in the example of the
salesperson. You often have to make cost/benefit decisions to
determine if the tolls you must pay to reach your career goals
are truly worth the price to you. In the next illustration, you
can see the tolls that this individual had to pay along the way to
his or her career destinations.

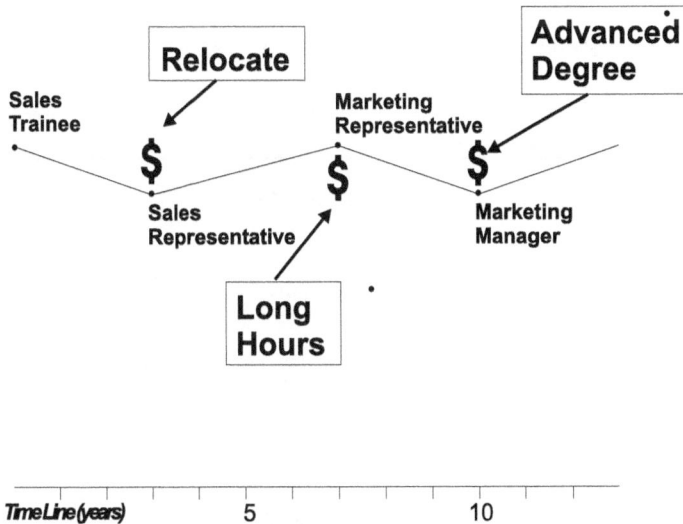

65

What Tolls Have You Had to Pay?

To help you better understand the "tolls" along your career roads, answer the following questions:

What "tolls" have you "paid" on your career roads?

What have been the rewards and benefits of paying these tolls?

Have these tolls been worth the price?

Do you know what the next tolls are to reach your career goals?

Are you willing to pay these tolls to get there?

Sign Posts

In the continuing example of the salesperson, signs have been placed on the career roads. These signs serve many of the same purposes as those found along a highway: they tell us where we are and where we are going. They warn us of roadblocks or hazards ahead. They often tell us how we should proceed.

Career road signs help us see which roads we can travel the fastest and which roads are most difficult to travel. They let us know when we are entering an area where the results take a long time to see. They warn us of dangerous intersections and caution us about traveling in directions away from our career goals. These signs tell us the type of road we are on and when we are nearing our career goals. In the example of the salesperson, the career road signs might look something like the example shown below. May times, signs are all around us but we do not see them or do not know how to read them correctly.

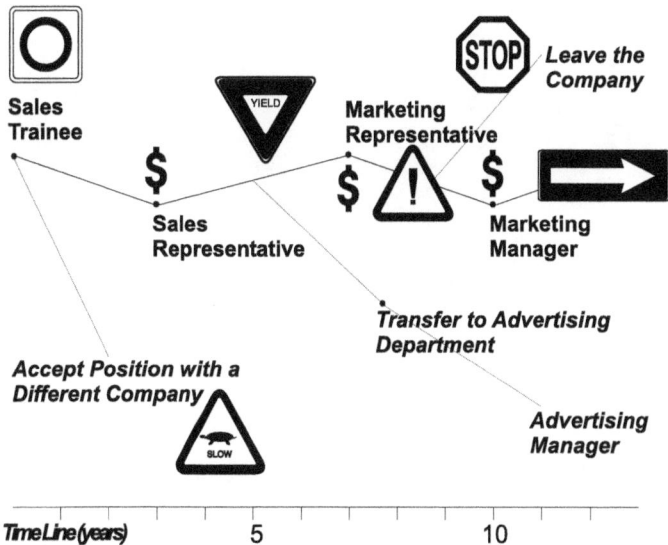

67

What Are Your Signs?

What are some of the signs you have read along your career roads?

What are some of the signs you might have missed or ignored?

What crossroads, detours or roadblocks might you encounter in the future?

Add the appropriate road signs to your career road map.

Conditions

Travel conditions can greatly affect a journey. Business climates, company policies, internal and external competition, economic conditions, technology and many other factors can influence your career. Sometimes it is fair and clear; conditions such as organizational growth and career opportunities can make your journey smoother, faster, and more enjoyable. Like the weather, there is often very little one can do about many of these conditions and, also like the weather, these conditions are constantly changing. Therefore, it is important that you keep informed about existing and anticipated conditions as you travel along your career roads. You may even have to take certain detours or alternative routes along the way to avoid the existing conditions that may stop your career progress.

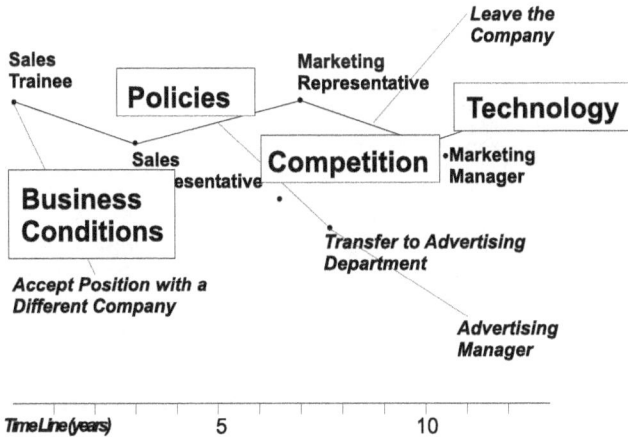

Sales Trainee

Policies

Marketing Representative

Leave the Company

Technology

Sales esentative

Competition

Marketing Manager

Business Conditions

Accept Position with a Different Company

Transfer to Advertising Department

Advertising Manager

TimeLine (years)   5   10

What Have Been Your Conditions?

What are some of the "uncontrollable" conditions that have affected your career?

How might you have prepared for or handled some of them more effectively?

How are you preparing for those that might occur in the future?

What compromises or trade-offs have you had to make during your career because of the prevailing conditions along your career roads?

Where have some of these career detours taken you that you would not have gone to otherwise?

Do you think that you are in a better place as a result? Why or why not?

If you have been detoured, how can you get back on track to the career roads that you would like to travel in the future?

Mapping Your Career Roads

Now draw a map of your career journey to this point, as you
see it, including your likely or chosen destination, directions,
tolls, signposts and conditions along the way. Place an arrow at
the point in the journey where you are today and label it,
"YOU ARE HERE."   Feel free to use colors on your map to
help illustrate your career journey. You will find it helpful to
refer back to your Career Map as you read the following
chapters of this book.

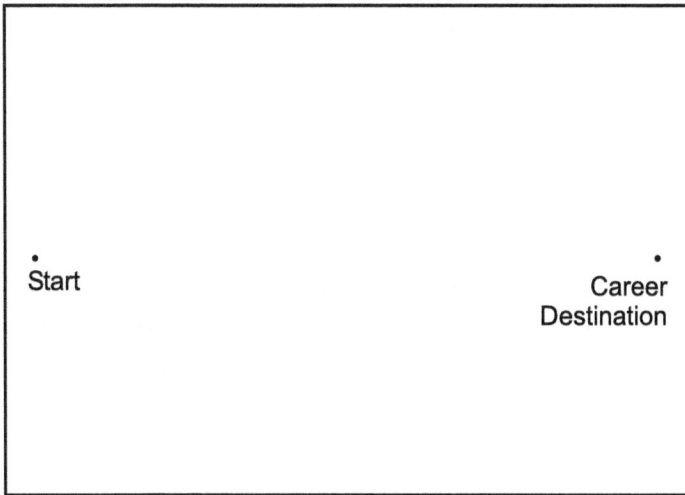

```
•
Start                                        •
                                          Career
                                          Destination
```

When Bad Things Happen to Good Careers

Bad things do happen to good careers. These bad things may have nothing to do with anything that the individual did or could have controlled. But they happen just the same. How one reacts to such a situation or event has as much to do with the negative and residual effects of the bad event as the event itself. Below are ways to deal with bad things that might happen during your career.

Remember That This Is Only a Career

In the event of an actual emergency, you will be notified of specific survival instructions. You need to keep your job in its proper perspective in terms of life crises. There are many worse things that can happen to you in your life than having a setback in your career. Sure, you need your job to support yourself and perhaps your family, but remember that a job is replaceable. Careers have highs and lows as part of the natural ebb and flow of your life. You may be in a low period at the moment but better days are surely ahead, particularly if you work towards achieving that end.

Don't Internalize Career Problems

This will only make things worse. This is, of course, easier said than done but you need to try to separate yourself from your career. Remember that your career is a role that you play in life. It may identify you to the outside world but it shouldn't define you as a person. Don't let events in your career change your self-perceptions. You will still be you when your career is over.

Things Change

What may seem like the most pressing crisis today may be but a mere afterthought tomorrow. Don't get all distraught over a problem or even a crisis that you may be involved in today, as it will eventually be resolved and you will move on to some other crisis of the day.

Careers Can Be Revitalized at Any Time

Like a prizefighter getting up off the mat before being counted out, careers can be resurrected. Often career success, or the lack thereof, is as much a function of situation as it is anything else. No matter how much of a beating your career may have endured, it is probably much more resilient than you give it credit for. It is much tougher than you may think.

Look at the Problem as an Opportunity

If you are given lemons, make lemonade. Make the most of the situation. As a response to the bad things that just happened, learn as much as you can to prevent them from recurring in the future. Or take this opportunity to make that change that you have been contemplating for so long. You never know what the unintended consequences of the situation may bring. You may just end up in a better position than you were in before.

Chapter Summary

In reality, your career roads never really end. There is always going to be another turn in the road, another crossroads to encounter during your career. You may not always reach the destinations that you thought you would when you first began the journey. However, you may discover that the journey is often more meaningful than the goals you originally dreamed of achieving. These are the experiences of a lifetime and as a result of them, you will discover things about yourself as well as other people that you never would have imagined. Make the most of the journey and be willing to be surprised along the way. It makes the journey so much more interesting.

CHAPTER FOUR

Pack Politics

On at least some level, organizational politics plays a critical role in everyone's career. To deny this is a mistake, one that is unfortunately made by many frustrated workers. You may not like organizational politics and may even try to avoid it, but it is very influential in your career.

In truth, organizational politics is something that most people would prefer to ignore. Everyone is aware that organizational politics exists, but most people probably spend little or no time trying to understand what it is really all about. However, much of what often frustrates people at work very likely has as much to do with organizational politics as with any other challenges or problems they face each day.

Organizational politics is not a new concept or even a fad but something that will always be part of going to work each day for anyone who is employed. Organizational politics exists in every organization. It is really just a matter of degree. You don't necessarily have to like or agree with organizational politics, but you do have to live with it and play the game, at least to some extent. This chapter is designed to help you understand the *pack politics* in your organization and be better able to deal with it more effectively in the future. It will help you look at organizational politics in new ways, changing how you think about it and its influence on your future and career. This book will even introduce you to a few new terms on this subject!

The Rat Race Is Full of Politics

Organizational politics refers to all of those influences at work that really have little or nothing to do with the quality of one's work but nevertheless can play an important role in determining its success. Organizational politics can seem to be completely out of one's control yet still has a tremendous influence on many important aspects of a person's career. Organizational politics by its very nature isn't necessarily fair or equitable. It knows no boundaries and can strike anyone at any time at any level of the organization. Consequently, organizational politics can be a very frustrating experience, especially if you are not a very good "politician" at work. Employees who work hard to do a good job may see their efforts completely negated due to the influence of organizational politics. This might occur because the boss was more interested in seeing someone else succeed or simply because the projects they were working on weren't top priorities of some other influential person in the organization. Whatever the case, it is critically important that you have a good understanding of what organizational politics is all about and its potential influence on your success.

Not paying enough attention to organizational politics is like performing all of the necessary steps to complete a task except one. However, in this case that one step that may have been skipped was a critically important one. It can cancel out all of the other efforts and good work that has previously been completed. But organizational politics doesn't have to be a negative thing. It can help you as well. This book will enable you to find better ways to make organizational politics work for you. You can turn what was once an obstacle or even a barrier to your success into a valuable asset to you in the future. However, this cannot be a passive experience on your part. You can't sit this one out and simply hope it will go away. Organizational politics will always be a powerful energy force in every workplace. You need to have this force working in your favor and best interest rather than against you. It is like Yoda said to Luke Skywalker in the ever-popular sci-fi movie *Star Wars*, "May the Force be with you!"

The Black Magic of Rat Race Politics

In the Rat Race at Work, organizational politics is by its very nature very confusing to most people. Organizational politics doesn't have to follow the same rules of reason and logic that are expected of other decisions made at work. It simply doesn't have to make sense. Organizational politics is allowed to break the rules, to go contrary to popular opinion, to fly in the face of company policy and even to be contradictory to past practices and procedures. In short, it can do anything it damn well pleases! The sooner you accept this fact, the better equipped you will be to deal with organizational politics in the future. Organizational politics will exist with or without your agreement or permission. Simply not agreeing with the organizational politics that may exist at your place of work won't make it go away. Like it or not, resist it as much as you can, stand your ground as much as your determination will allow, there will still be organizational politics where you work.

Organizational politics can seem like a mysterious journey into the unknown. It can be the ultimate "black box" that few (if any) truly understand or can control. It may even appear to many employees that decisions made under its influence are a result of secret incantations recited by the top management of the organization. One can almost picture what goes on behind those closed boardroom doors. Images of bubbling, boiling cauldrons of mysterious decisions being brewed in secret passageways of the executive suites come to mind as everyone in the organization anxiously awaits the next politically motivated edict to be decreed. The potion of what goes into these dark decisions might consist of something like the eye of a toad, ear of a lizard, head of the Treasurer, neck of the Vice-president and soul of the Human Resources Director. And in many ways, this may not be that far from the truth!

Organizational politics on some level is part of every process involving people from kindergarten children playing in the schoolyard to the billion-dollar decisions made in corporate executive boardrooms. Again, it is all just a matter of degree and scale. Think back to when you were in kindergarten. Wasn't there a circumstance when either your teacher or your parents made some decision that didn't make sense to you even at your young and tender age at that time? Maybe it was another child that you were told not to play with or the classmate who got to be Hall Monitor or was assigned the coveted job of erasing the blackboard chalk or whatever. This may have been one of your very first experiences with organizational politics. This decision probably didn't make any more sense to you then than many of the politically motivated decisions that may be affecting you at work today. You may have received no more logical or understandable answer to your question, "Why does Suzy always get to be Hall Monitor?" from your kindergarten teacher than you got to your question, "Why didn't I get that promotion?" from your employer today. Suzy may have gotten this prestigious assignment because her father was active in the PTA or her mother was on the local Board of Directors of the school. Or maybe Suzy just was a bigger "suck-up" than everyone else in the class!

Whatever the case, you probably felt like pulling Suzy's hair or dipping one of her pigtails in green oil-based paint during art class. Maybe you would like to do these things to

79

someone at your place of employment? Maybe you had better hold back this urge for the time being until you have read the rest of this chapter and have learned how to channel these feelings concerning organizational politics at your workplace in more positive ways!

And so it goes. Like it or not, politics is indeed part of every aspect of our lives and is certainly part of the Rat Race at Work. Yes, we're stuck with it, so we might as well try to understand what it's all about and how we can deal with it better in the future. No matter how childish it may sometimes seem to be, it is really very serious business. It can significantly affect careers, fortunes and even fate itself. It will probably exist on some level in every decision that is made in your organization. Your future may be as much influenced by organizational politics as by any other factor in your career. Thus this is a very important subject to understand better. This is not to say that the quality of one's hard work and efforts are not critically important or will always automatically be superseded by some political factor in the organization— quite the contrary. Organizational politics is simply a reality that everyone, regardless of his or her status or stature in the company, must heed to an appropriate degree. This enhanced understanding of organizational politics, together with one's hard work and talents, is the best combination for a successful career.

Although everyone can probably think of circumstances that contradict this next statement, it is still generally true that just focusing on the politics that occur in an organization is not enough to be successful. Politics is not a legitimate substitute for qualifications, hard work and talent in a job. Those who attempt to use or manipulate organizational politics as a replacement for these principles will not be successful in the long term. Sooner or later the political factions that may previously have been supporting them will no longer be valid. Without these connections they no longer have the ability to ride these political waves or be buffered and protected by these political influences. Although it may seem incredibly unfair at times, organizational politics has a way of equalizing its influence in the long run. Life ultimately is fair. No one (with a few exceptions) gets out of some amount of hard work and is totally protected and carried throughout his or her career on organizational politics alone. No one gets to ride completely for free.

So it is this balance of talent, qualifications, hard work, experience, etc., combined with a good understanding of the influence of the organizational politics, that is the formula for success that we are seeking. It may be like those mysterious magical potions brewing in the executive boardroom that we want to learn more about. Just what amount of each of these important and valuable ingredients do we need in this magical formula for success?

The following exercise will help you get closer to the answer to this age-old question. But as is so often said in situations like this in the past, the answers to these questions must be discovered for yourself. It is only then that you will truly understand and appreciate the significance of their meaning.

Organizational Politics Detector

Wouldn't it be wonderful to have a tool that told you exactly what part of any decision made in your organization was politically oriented and motivated and what was free of these influences? Unfortunately, such a precise instrument doesn't yet exist. However, you can begin to get a better understanding of just how much organizational politics exists in a given situation or decision by thinking about these events differently. The following Organizational Politics Detector will help you sniff out these circumstances and will better guide you concerning what actions you should take and what influence you can have over the situation. Of course, like just about anything else that you buy today, there is some assembly required.

Assembly and Instructions

Step 1 - The first thing you need to do to assemble your Organizational Politics Detector is to take it out of the box. In other words, you need to start thinking about organizational politics more often and be more conscious of its existence.

Step 2 - The next thing you need to do is to activate your Organizational Politics Detector. All of us have our own built-in Organizational Politics Detector. It is just that some people have exercised and developed their detectors more than others. Just like our muscles, it tends to atrophy without use. Or like other innate talents that you might have, it doesn't do you any good unless you practice and use it. In other words, you need to be constantly looking for the possibility or the existence of organizational politics in just about everything that happens at work. The more you use your Organizational Politics Detector, the more useful it will become.

Step 3 - Become familiar with the sounds that organizational politics makes when it appears. There should be a little alarm that goes off in your head alerting you to the possibility that organizational politics is at work again. Beep, beep, beep . . . your Organizational Politics Detector is going off again. You need to identify what organizational politics sounds like in your organization. It can frequently be identified by what is referred to as the *politically correct* thing to say.

Step 4 - Be prepared for updates to your Organizational Politics Detector. Like a computer program, your Organizational Politics Detector will need to be updated from time to time to keep up with the latest changes that are taking place in the organizational politics at your place of work. Unfortunately, you won't be receiving these changes automatically on-line through the modem in your computer. These are updates that you will have to discover for yourself. Organizational politics can take on different forms as it is constantly evolving and reinventing itself. Don't always expect it to look and sound the same. Often just when you think you have finally figured it out or at least have begun to understand how it operates, it will completely change. It's like one of those old low-budget monster films where every time the scientists try to destroy the creature it appears in a different form. Organizational Politics can behave in very similar ways. You can't kill it or destroy it, only change its appearances and form.

Now let's test how well your Organizational Politics Detector may be working with the following exercise called

"When they say _____, they really mean. _____." You may want to turn up the volume on your detector to ensure that you can hear when it begins to beep.

Playing the "When They Say _____" Exercise

This exercise is easy to play. All you do is simply answer the second part of each question with what you think is the *real* meaning of each statement.

Here's an example: When they say something like, "*In order to meet our company's overall strategic mission and profitability goals, we are implementing this new program to cut costs by X%,*" what this statement really means is . . . "*The company didn't meet its financial goals again last quarter and the top executives are getting a lot of pressure from stockholders to do something to stop the financial bleeding going on in the organization.*" Your Organizational Politics Detector should be going off about now: Beep, beep, beep!

To get you sarted, the next few examples will provide the first part of a potentially politically correct statement that might be heard in a typical organization. You need to fill in the blanks with what you feel is the real meaning of the statement. The last few examples provide you with the opportunity to identify both the politically correct statement and its real meaning from your own experiences.

When they say, *"In order to streamline the efficiencies of our operations, we are exploring alternatives concerning several of our facilities,"* what this really means is:

_____

_____

When they say, *"Someone has left the organization to explore other career opportunities,"* what this really means is:

_____

_____

When they say, *"Due to poor financial results during the past fiscal year, associates should have realistic expectations concerning compensation next year,"* what this really means is:

_____

_____

When they say, *"We are looking into other possibilities concerning the continued investment of resources into this aspect of our operations,"* what this really means is:

_____

_____

When they say, *"We are looking at realigning our business portfolio to help us be more competitive in the future,"* what this really means is:

_____

_____

When they say, *"We recognize just how hard all of you are working today to help make our organization successful. However, we are still falling short of our performance goals and must work together to meet these important but difficult challenges ahead. We are not asking you to work harder—just smarter—in the future to reach these goals,"* what this really means is:

_____

_____

Now create both parts of the exercise yourself by filling in the blanks for both the politically correct statement and its real meaning, based on your own experiences.

When they say

_____

What this really means is:

_____

When they say

_____

What this really means is:

_____

When they say

_____

What this really means is:

_____

When they say

_____

What this really means is:

_____

When they say

_____

What this really means is:

_____

When they say

_____

What this really means is:

_____

Organizational Politics Formula

> All other factors (resources, conditions, environment, people, etc.)
>
> x   Organizational Political Influencers (Impact)
>
> ─────────────────────────────────────
>
> =   Decision/Action

This formula can help you better understand how much of any decision or action is based on organizational politics rather than on other factors independent of its influence. Although not a precisely accurate instrument, it can still give you a better picture of the influence of organizational politics than you would have without it. It is important to note that as you work through this formula, one thing you will quickly realize is that there are a number of factors that contribute to any decision or action in addition to any organizational politics that might come into play. As shown in the formula, these factors may consist of the *resources* that are currently available, including capital; the *conditions* that presently exist, in which any decisions must be made; the *environment* in which decisions are made, including what is happening in the business and markets the organization must compete with; and, last but certainly not least, the *people* affected by the decision.

All of these factors, as well as others, are impacted by the influence of organizational politics. Organizational politics' influence can significantly vary depending on any number of reasons. This variation can be called the *organizational politics impact.* This impact can be strong or it can be relatively weak. Impact can be described as similar to the concept of multipliers in math. A multiplier may be low; for example, it could be a factor of 1. This means that it basically has little or no impact. Organizational politics can be the same way. However, in other circumstances it can have a significant impact. It could be a factor of 10 or even more. In this circumstance, organizational politics would have a tremendous influence on the ultimate decision. Regardless of its impact, it often seems that whenever organizational politics appears it takes on an even greater influence. Contact with organizational politics can be a very emotional experience for those directly affected by its influence, making it seem bigger than it sometimes really is. Often, organizational politics is ascribed more credit than it earns, blamed for more things than it actually causes, and given a bum rap that it doesn't deserve!

Using the Organizational Politics Formula

To use the formula, you need to begin by identifying the factors that would contribute to the decision other than those influenced by organizational politics. These are the factors that go into the first part of the formula. These factors might include those described in the formula (Resources, Conditions, Environment and People), but may also involve other factors as well. These are for you to identify. Next you need to identify what organizational politics may be part of the decision-making process. Organizational politics is defined for this purpose as all of those influencers at work that really have little or nothing to do with the factors listed in the first part of the formula but can nevertheless play an important role in determining the success or outcome of the decision. Finally, you need to determine the impact or multiplier effect of these organizational politics. As explained above, an impact of 1 would have little or no influence on the ultimate decision. An impact of 2 or more would begin to significantly change the decision.

Let's look at an example. Let's say that the following circumstances existed in an organization: The company is experiencing a decline in their business due to increased competition for their product in the marketplace. There have been a number of negative consequences to this situation, including a steep decline in the price of the company's stock over the past several months. The Board of Directors of the company is greatly concerned about these declines and has put pressure on the CEO to do something about this situation immediately. Much of their remuneration for serving on the company's board is in the form of bonuses paid as stock options. Unfortunately for these board members, these options are not very attractive at the current price of the company's stock. They have made it clear to the CEO and other top officials in the company that their support for them to continue in their current roles in the organization is contingent on their ability to remedy this situation. In response, the CEO has initiated a realignment of the organization in hopes of being better able to react aggressively to this situation, resulting in a number of new assignments of employees. He has made it clear that his top priority is to regain the market share that the company has recently lost. He has also made it known that any projects or proposals that come across his desk that don't contribute in a significant way to this objective will not be approved.

Now let's look at this situation in relation to the formula:

All other factors (resources, conditions, environment, people, etc.)

x   Organizational Political Influencers (Impact)

=   Decision/Action

Say that a manager in the organization sends a request to the CEO to hire additional people for a project that he would like to initiate. This project, although potentially beneficial to the organization, does not directly impact the competitive situation that currently exists. These factors would be multiplied by the organizational political influences currently in existence. In this case the impact would be significant—let's say a factor of 10. Therefore, the formula would look something like this:

Request for additional people for a project not directly impacting competitive situation

x   Organization's desire to address the competitive situation (multiplied by a factor of 10)

=   Denial of the request

Seen in this manner, the answer that the formula would produce is very obvious and easy to predict. But what is the real political motivator that is driving the decision that the formula produced? There are many possible factors, but based on what we know in this scenario it appears that the primary driver is the bonuses for the members of the company's Board of Directors. This is how the mystery and black magic of organizational politics is often created. Although everyone in the organization can relate to the need to address this decline in business, the real driver in this situation may not be so easily understood.

It is unlikely that the remedy described above will be the only action taken by top management of the organization to deal with this situation. They may see other actions taken in an attempt to placate the members of the Board of Directors, including ones that do not make any sense to them. Programs or initiatives may be designed to show the board that the competitive problem is being addressed, and some will be approved for this explicit reason even if they do not actually serve that purpose. For example, highly visible campaigns such as letters to employees, banners, slogans, etc. may be endorsed at the expense of other proposals, such as the request for additional people to handle another problem that is important but not directly related to the politically charged issue.

This situation occurs because the highly visible projects may give the members of the board the impression that their concerns are being addressed, even though these resources could be better spent on something else. No wonder organizational politics can be so confusing! Beep, beep, beep.

Gaining this better understanding of what organizational politics is really all about is the subject of the next section, Defining Organizational Politics. As the brief example above illustrates, identifying organizational politics is one thing, but truly understanding it can be an entirely new and different challenge in itself!

Defining Organizational Politics

Understanding just what organizational politics is all about is often as great a challenge as dealing with it once identified. Just what is the nature of this political beast in the Rat Race at Work that we must constantly be dealing with each day at work? This can be an elusive beast that can often change shape and form in an instant. It can slip through the tiniest opening or where one doesn't even exist, and it typically appears without invitation or welcome. It is a complex beast—sometimes cruel and vicious, sometimes kind and forgiving. It can appear to some to be a hideously ugly creature and to others beautiful and appealing. Even stranger is that two people can come into contact with this same beast and have vastly different experiences. How can people have encounters with the same set of political circumstances and factors and yet come away with totally different reactions? How can they be talking about the same thing with such diverse perceptions?

The answer to all of the above questions has to do with perceptions. Truth truly is a point of view. It is really a matter of how you want to see the truth that influences your perceptions of it as much as anything else. Perception is reality to the person experiencing it. There can be no absolute definition of organizational politics because it is different for each person. The greatest differential is how a person is affected by organizational politics. This is where this perceptual ambidexterity comes into play. Each of us sees organizational politics through our own experiences or, to use a photography metaphor, through our own lens. We each get a different picture of organizational politics and frame it in different ways based upon our own realities.

It is like that famous drawing of a woman that can be seen in several different ways. If you look at it from one perspective, you see a young and stylish lady, but viewed another way the woman looks like an old hag. The difference is a matter of one's perception. There is really no right or wrong way of looking at the picture, as is also the case with organizational politics. It is more a function of how one is affected by organizational politics that determines perceptions and, ultimately, reality to that individual. *Fair* is truly a four-letter word that can be quite profane to someone who feels that he got the short end of the stick, so to speak.

To begin to understand organizational politics, it is necessary to understand what it is not. An obvious analogy might be made to our nation's political system, but this is *not* a good comparison for organizational politics. Although there are some similarities (for example, there is a great deal of hot air expended in the form of rhetoric in both systems!), there are more differences than commonalties.

On the fairness issue, even our national political system has organizational politics beat hands down! Organizational politics has no elections or re-elections, no political platforms, no voting records of legislators to compare or judge, no balance of power, no two-party system, no justice department to enforce rules or establish consistency, not even an impeachment process. The only similarity may be both systems' propensity for scandal!

Organizations in which people are employed are not intended to be democracies. All employees are not considered to be equals and there are no inalienable rights decreed in organizational politics. An organization is a closed system that for the most part creates its own rules and plays by them as well. Fairness is not necessarily the ultimate objective in this game, and people can and do get hurt in the organizational political process. This is the way the Rat Race at Work can seem to be such an unfair condition. The winners are not always the ones who crossed the finish line first or even close to the leaders of the pack.

A term often used to describe a phenomenon that frequently occurs in our national political system is *pork barrel politics*. Politicians need to keep their voters' interests in mind when performing their jobs either in their state capitals or in Washington. Pork barrel refers to special interests that certain groups of constituents might have back home. Pork barrel politics may involve compromise, deal making, trade-offs and just about any other tactic imaginable to ensure the passing of certain legislation that benefits some special interest group. It is often argued that pork barrel politics doesn't always serve the needs of the whole but rather only those of these special interest groups. Pork barrel gets money spent on projects in a politician's community, district or state. These funds might be spent more wisely on other more appropriate and necessary projects and programs that better serve society as a whole. But the reality is that these special interest groups are often successful in obtaining funding that really doesn't make any sense to anyone except those who are directly benefited. Pork barrel politics often causes millions and even billions of dollars to be spent each year on projects that serve the interests of only a relatively few. Most often it is more a function of their elected official's ability to secure these public monies than the actual need or justification of the project. This could be argued to be our national political process at both its best and its worst.

The equivalent of pork barrel politics in organizations might be called *board barrel politics*. Board barrel politics refers to this same type of special interest or pet project favoritism that might exist in an organization's political process. This is one area in which the national and organizational political systems can be very similar. Board barrel politics can be a very powerful influence in organizations. Board barrel politics is not intended to be a derogatory term about these important decision makers in an organization. There is no question that they play a crucial role in the future of an organization. Much of an organization's success or failure is based on the decisions they make and their vision of the future. Board barrel politics doesn't just refer to what the Board of Directors or other important decision makers in an organization might want to happen in the organization but also to what others might think they want. There is a difference between these two, often a huge one. This difference can be as great as the gap between perceptions and reality.

The following short story describes how board barrel politics works in a typical organization. The story illustrates the impact that the board barrel politics of one important and powerful person can have on the entire organization or, in this case, the perceptions that others have of what the boss really wants!

Political Games

Jim Miller had worked his way to the top from very humble beginnings. Twenty-five years ago, he had begun his career as an hourly worker in one of the company's manufacturing facilities that happened to be located in the small town where he had been born and raised. Jim hadn't really intended to become a leader or even dreamed that he could ever be more than an hourly worker. But leadership was just something that seemed to come naturally to him. His fellow workers, recognizing his natural leadership abilities, had recruited him to run for president of their local union to represent their interests better than their leadership had in the past. He was elected to the top position of the local union by an overwhelming margin over the incumbent president.

Jim didn't disappoint them, either. He fought hard to have their problems and issues heard by management and was successful in effecting significant improvements for everyone. After a particularly difficult contract negotiation with the company in which Jim was able to successfully negotiate sizable increases in wages and benefits for the union membership, there were more than a few executives in the organization who were very impressed with him. "This is one person I want to have on our side from now on!" the head of the company's labor relations group was heard to say after sitting across from Jim at the bargaining table. It wasn't very long before they offered him a management job. With the encouragement of family and friends, Jim somewhat reluctantly accepted the job and the challenges that it brought. He came to realize that he could make even greater contributions to those he had worked so hard for during his tenure as president of the local union in this new and challenging position now being offered to him.

However, Jim soon learned just how much more complicated leadership could be than what he had experienced as president of a relatively small union local. He had not been adequately prepared for the organizational politics that would exist on the management levels at which he now found himself. Sure, there were constant favors being asked of him as a union official. One employee would put pressure on him to make sure his grievance was presented before someone else's or different people would want their issues presented during contract negotiations. He understood all of these issues and was able to put each of them in their proper perspective and priority. However, there were pressures and influences in his new position that he didn't begin to understand. Things just weren't as clear-cut as they used to be in his former life, to which he often found himself longing to return.

He learned that things weren't always as they may first appear. As an hourly worker he could expect that what someone said they wanted and what they really wanted were the same thing. However, this was not always the case in the executive boardrooms of the company. Everything in this new environment seemed to require a certain amount of investigation. He also learned that he needed to understand what the real issues were behind what people said. As he followed these "issue trails," they typically all led to the same place: the office of one of the top executives of the corporation. It was amazing just how much of the desires and expectations of these powerful individuals drove the entire organization. At first, it was kind of fun trying to uncover the real meaning behind all the memos and speeches. It reminded him of the games he played as a kid growing up back home. Only now the consequences of these games were much greater than whose turn it was to hide or what number of fingers were hidden behind someone's back. Now the organizational political games were serious business. People's careers and futures were dependent on the outcomes.

Despite this initial confusion, he learned how to navigate his way through the obstacles that organizational politics presented. His characteristic persuasive personality and charm allowed him to rise quickly to greater levels of responsibility and power. He even learned to play political games himself and eventually became quite skilled in these maneuvers. He thought of organizational politics as if it were one big poker game. Sometimes you could get by through simply bluffing that you were holding good cards and sometimes you really did have good cards. It was all a matter of what cards other people thought you had.

After just a short time in his new role as part of the management of the organization, Jim Miller discovered the absolute power of organizational politics. It was an energy force greater than any single person in the organization, even the CEO. He found circumstances when outside influences quickly changed the political agendas of even the most influential members of the company's executive officers. He saw even the most elaborate and detailed corporate policies and tactics quickly change as these outside influences altered the political landscape of the company and the strategic direction in which the company was headed.

Jim also discovered that among the most powerful influences in an organization were the wishes and desires of some higher-ranking officials of the company. He also learned that it was not only important what one of these executive wanted but also just as important what everyone else thought this influential person wanted. He found that simply dropping the name of an important person in association with a project he was working on could do wonders regarding everyone's motivation to help complete the assignment. This was where his experience as a poker player was very helpful. He had known that someday those Friday night poker games with the boys back home would pay off! He never intentionally deceived anyone concerning whose pet project he was working on, but he didn't worry too much if someone somehow got the wrong impression about who was really sponsoring or advocating the project.

Adding to this confusion was the fact that everyone just automatically associated Jim with the higher-ranking officials of the company. Jim was often given the responsibility of carrying out the wishes of the top executives of the company. They had quickly learned that they could depend on Jim to get things accomplished in the "real world" of the company's manufacturing operations. After all, that was where he had his roots and that was what he knew best. He had risen from the ranks because of his innate ability to work the system. Now this was the skill that the top management of the company wanted him to provide for them. Jim was now one of their best resources for fulfilling their own political agendas in the environment that he understood better than any of them. Political assets can mean many different things to many different people. It all depends on the perspectives and positions from which you see things.

Jim learned that the most important seven words in the organization were, "This is what Bob wants to do." The Bob in this case was Robert Blackwell, the Vice-president of Manufacturing who ran the operations of the company with an iron fist. Even the mention of his name invoked fear in anyone who was part of his organization. Jim quickly learned that this fact could be an excellent method for fulfilling the wishes of Bob, which was something that he worked hard to do. Most disagreements about what course of action to follow within Blackwell's organization were settled by someone's saying those words, "This is what Bob wants to do." And that someone uttering these words more often than not was Jim.

In truth, Jim Miller despised organizational politics. It smacked of everything he hated. He believed that a person or an idea should stand on merit alone and not on how good a fit there was with someone's political agenda. But he also was a realist. He knew that to ignore the organizational politics that existed at any given time in a situation would be a huge mistake. He did worry about how his old friends at the factory back home would think of him when he was forced into going along with certain politically motivated ideas or actions. He still kept in touch with his old friends and found himself constantly trying to educate them about how politics worked in the organization. He could tell that they didn't completely buy into the supposed logic behind such things as organizational politics and maybe even thought less of him for playing along with these games. Of course, they would never say anything to him about these feelings. They knew they had a great advocate in Jim to promote their local issues to the upper management of the company and didn't want to alienate him. In truth, they were playing the same political game as Jim.

Discussion Questions

What political games did you see in the story about Jim Miller's rise from hourly worker to corporate executive?

Do you think that these games were justifiable? In other words, do you think that Jim had "sold out" in order to move ahead in the company? Why or why not?

Do you think that Jim was right in his belief that he could help his friends in the factory more as part of management than as their union president, or was he just interested in his own career advancement? Why or why not?

Do you agree that Jim's buddies back home were playing the same political game that Jim was playing, as indicated in the story? Why or why not?

The Biggie Rat

In the preceding story, Robert Blackwell was the CEO, or in other words the *Biggie Rat* in the pack. How well you get along with the Biggie Rat in your organization can play an important role in your career. Again, like organizational politics, often it is not always *what* you know but *who* you know. This does not imply that you should compromise your values or principles or become the biggest "suck-up" to the boss in the office. But it does mean that you can't afford to ignore completely this fact of organizational dynamics that does have a significant influence on your success in the Rat Race at Work. Dealing with the Biggie Rat in your organization, whoever that may be, needs to be part of your overall strategy for success in your career.

10 Biggie Rat Strategies

Below are tips on dealing with the Biggie Rat(s) in your organization. Feel free to modify them to fit your own situation and circumstance. Everyone needs to work from his or her own style and comfort zones, especially when dealing with the Biggie Rats of the world.

1. **Relax around Biggie Rat**. Remember that Biggie Rat was once just one of the pack like you. Even the Biggie Rat eats his or her cheese just like anyone else. Even though it may not always seem like it, Biggie Rat is not royalty or divinity. Thinking of Biggie Rat in more realistic terms can help you be more comfortable and effective in your dealings with him or her.

2. **Always be prepared.** Think about what he or she might ask you and have answers or comments prepared. To do this, think about what the Biggie Rat is interested in rather than what your own interests are. Good guesses as to what this might be are the critical issues facing the organization today. The boss will most likely ask you questions or ask for your opinion to better understand the result of his or her decisions. Keep in mind that Biggie Rat has a boss of his or her own. Biggie Rat's boss will be someone even more powerful in the organization or could even be the Chair of the Board of Directors. Everyone has to answer to someone else. Find out what issues the Biggie Rat's boss might want to know about and you can anticipate what might be asked of you. Remember that pressure to achieve results usually flows downhill in an organization. This is one thing that Biggie Rat is more than willing to share with you.

3. **Be in control.** Strive to give the impression to Biggie Rat that you are in control of your job and accountabilities. Biggie Rat has enough to worry about without becoming concerned that you are not in control of your area of responsibilities. Avoid the temptation to tell Biggie Rat about all the problems you are facing on your job just so he or she is forewarned. Instead, share the solutions you are implementing. This makes a much better impression and allows Biggie Rat to sleep better at night

4. **Always have an "elevator speech" prepared.** You never know when you might find yourself in one of those unexpected occasions when you are suddenly face to face with Biggie Rat. Don't waste these opportunities for exposure to Biggie Rat on chitchat or small talk. Always have conceptualized in your mind a quick summary of what you are working on or your latest accomplishment, ready to be presented in the amount of time it takes for an elevator to travel a few floors and the doors to open.

5. **Provide summary information.** Give Biggie Rat summarized information, not the encyclopedia version. Remember that Biggie Rat has tons of information that he or she must digest all the time. More is not necessarily better in this case. Pick the most important points that you want Biggie Rat to know and present them in the form of clear, crisp bullet points. Biggie Rat will tell you if he or she wants more detail, and be prepared to provide these particulars upon request.

6. **Don't be afraid to express your opinion.** Biggie Rats don't typically want to have a pack of "yes-rats" working for them. Biggie Rats need to understand the opinions and perspectives of the organization. Biggie Rats by virtue of their position can become isolated from the rest of the pack. They need to be brought back to reality from time to time. But also be careful when delivering a message that is not in alignment with the Biggie Rat's opinion or decision. While Biggie Rat may need to hear the message, beware of constantly being the bearer of bad news. The

ancient custom of shooting the messenger of bad news still exists in modern day terms. Biggie Rat might begin to think that what he or she needs is to get rid of the messenger rather than to accept the bad news.

7. **Don't talk about Biggie Rat behind his or her back.** Remember that bosses have big ears, especially Biggie Rats. What you say about the boss can come back to haunt you. It may not happen the next day but it can happen. Bad-mouthing the boss may be like setting a time bomb for yourself to get blasted by at some later point in time. Worse yet, don't put derogatory opinions about the boss in writing, in an email or on a voice mail message that can be stored or retrieved by someone who would like nothing better than to have one less person to compete against for the next promotion.

8. **Be aware of the "pet projects" of Biggie Rat.** Most bosses have certain projects or programs that they would especially like to see succeed. You need to know if you are currently assigned to such a project and ensure that it gets the attention that it deserves. You don't want to inadvertently ignore or shortchange a project or initiative that is important to Biggie Rat—that is, unless you are trying to get on his or her bad side.

9. **Know Biggie Rat's background.** Be aware of where Biggie Rat worked before becoming the *big cheese*. This will tell you a great deal about how he or she will approach the problems of today. It

gives you a big clue as to Biggie Rat's approach to problem solving. For instance, if Biggie Rat came from a financial background, he or she may look for solutions to problems in the numbers. If Biggie Rat came from a sales or marketing background, the answers to the most pressing problems of the day may be customer-related. There are many ways to skin a cat, so to speak, and you need to be aware of how Biggie Rat might think it should be accomplished.

10. **Cut Biggie Rat a break (at least once in a while).** This may not always be easy. By the nature of their jobs, Biggie Rats of the world have to do many unpopular things. Or, the very personal characteristics that allow someone to move to the head of the pack may not always be the most congenial. Regardless, avoid falling into the common syndrome of becoming polarized from the boss. It is easy to disagree with what the boss wants to see done in the organization. There is always some mounting opposition to just about anything that the Biggie Rat is trying to accomplish. Remember, you may not know everything that the boss knows. If you did, you might be making the same decisions as him or her.

Chapter Summary

The Rat Race at Work is full of politics. Like it or not, organizational politics does play an important part in everyone's career. To deny this fact can be a big mistake to anyone interested in his or her career advancement. You may not agree with or like the pack politics that currently exists in your organization, but you do need to at least recognize the strong influence it has on the decisions that can affect your career. Developing a personal strategy to deal more effectively with these political forces, especially in regard to the Biggie Rat in your organization, will help you be more successful in Winning the Rat Race at Work. The next chapter will help you to develop strategies that will aid you in accomplishing these objective as well as other important career goals.

CHAPTER FIVE

Rat Race Planning

Unfortunately, most people don't have a career plan or strategy. Typically an individual will have certain goals in mind that he or she would like to reach in their career but no actual plan or strategy concerning how to reach these objectives. This is like starting out on an automobile trip without a destination in mind or a map to tell you how to get there. If you don't know where you are going, any road will get you there. This chapter will help you develop a career strategy to better visualize the journey that needs to be traveled as well as some diversions that might be encountered along the way.

Planning can be the most important step in anything that you try to do in your life. Planning can help you break down a large, complicated process into smaller steps that can help make a humongous job seem less overwhelming. Each step in the process becomes a milestone to be reached. You need to feel good about accomplishing each step along the way as you progress towards achieving your ultimate goal. This is particularly true when undertaking large projects for which the final results may be a long time coming. You need to celebrate the small stuff as well as the big. Your career deserves this same planning as well. You need to establish the milestones in your career that you want to achieve and recognize when you have reached these objectives. You need to reward yourself for each of the accomplishments you achieve during your career journey. And you need to have a vision of where each step is taking you along the career roads that you will travel.

Think Career Strategy

For just a moment, think about your career as unemotionally as you possibly can. In other words, try to separate your own personal feelings from your career. Granted, this may be difficult to do as you have such a vested interest in this process, but do the best you can to look at your career as objectively as possible. Now think of your career as you would any other important project that your boss, Biggie Rat or anyone else in your organization may assign you. How would you approach such a project? Most likely you would first sit down and create some sort of project plan that would provide a framework and timetable for accomplishing the major steps that need to be achieved in the process. Why wouldn't you use this same process when it comes to planning your career?

A career plan doesn't need to be complicated. It can involve a simple matrix that helps you identify the action items or milestones that you wish to reach during your career, the deliverables that will help you reach these milestones, what support you need to accomplish each of these goals, and the status of the goal. An example of a career plan matrix is shown below:

Your Career Plan

	Actions/Goals/ Milestones	Task (T) Goal (G)	Deliverables	Support	Due Date	Status
1.						
2.						
3.						
4.						
5.						
6.						
7.						
8.						
9.						
10.						
11.						
12.						
13.						
14.						
15.						
16.						
17.						
18.						
19.						
20.						
21.						
22.						
23.						
24.						
25.						

Instructions for Creating Your Career Plan

Below are explanations of the terms used as column headings in the Career Plan template on the preceding page. As you read through the descriptions, consider how each item applies to your particular career situation.

Actions/Goals/Milestones

As you would any other major project, you need to sit down and think about and visualize the entire process, including the final result that you expect to achieve. To help you identify these significant steps on your career journey, take another look at the Career Map that you developed in the previous chapter. The major career stops you identified along the way for the past, present and future can serve as *actions, goals, or milestones* for your Career Plan. But you shouldn't necessarily restrict yourself to just these points along your career roads. Also think about the things that you need to do in order to make these significant milestones happen. What are some of the major drivers that can get you where you want to go in your career? List as many of these action items or milestones that you can think of on your plan. You will identify those that are *tasks* and those that are *goals* in the next column, so don't worry about these differences at this point in the process.

Task/Goal

An important distinction for each action item or milestone is whether it is a *task*, designated by a T, or a *goal*, designated by a G. Tasks are actions that must be taken. Goals are objectives to be reached. For the purposes of this plan, think of goals as where you want to be in your career at key points in your journey. Again, your Career Map can help provide these data points. Think of tasks as what you need to do to reach each of these points. Both are critically important to the success of your career and must be identified from the very beginning of the process. If these important steps in the process are not clearly identified and included in the plan, the entire process will suffer. Many times, goals are not reached because these major steps in the process are not identified sequentially and put into an action-oriented plan.

Deliverables

Deliverables are just what their name implies: these are the things that must be done in order to reach the milestones, tasks, or goals described in the plan. Think of deliverables as the output of the process. This is what needs to be produced in order to stay on plan. Without deliverables, the plan will not be successful. Certain deliverables are more easily achieved than others but all of them are vitally important to the final outcome. You probably will spend most of your time during your career focused on producing these deliverables. This is why it is so important that they be clearly identified as early in any project as possible. You need to be focusing your energies and efforts on achieving these deliverables. Spending your time on other non-critical things that are not part of the project plan will only move you farther away from your goals and cause you to waste valuable resources as well as opportunities. The key to any project's success is to identify your deliverables and keep focused on achieving these objectives.

115

Support

For each action item or milestone that you want to achieve, you need to identify the *support* that you will need to accomplish the goal. This support may also be in the form of a *champion* who can help you achieve this objective. A champion can be anyone who can help you reach your objectives. A champion may also just provide support to you as you work towards your goal. This can also be of great benefit to you. Encouragement from a friend, mentor, peer, supervisor, or family member plays an important role in helping you stay focused on your ultimate career goals. It is important to identify this support early in the process. If you don't have the support necessary to achieve the goal, your chances of success are greatly diminished, possibly to zero. Make sure that you know where your support will come from, as well as where it might not exist.

Due Date

You need to set *due dates* by which you would like to reach each of the goals, actions or milestones and monitor your progress against these timetables. Setting dates to reach certain points in your career can help you remain focused on these targets and possibly drive accomplishments to be reached according to this schedule. This is one area of the plan that you may need to keep flexible. Careers don't always progress on the timetables or schedules that you may originally establish for yourself. Often goals are set extremely aggressively, particularly in the first stages of a career. Someone making the statement, "I expect to be the CEO within 10 years" may show great ambition and drive but may turn out to be unrealistic for any number of reasons. Don't carve your timetables in stone. You may find you need to adjust them based on circumstances often out of your control.

It is important to note that this same theme of flexibility should be remembered when developing the entire plan. Circumstances change throughout a career, including one's interests and goals. A career plan needs to be a dynamic process that is constantly adjusted to meet an individual's current plans and ambitions.

Status

Status refers to the current achievement level of the goal, action, or milestone. This can be expressed any number of ways. The simplest method is to list an estimated percentage of the goal, action, or milestone that has been completed. For instance, this entry may be 100%, 50%, 10% or any other fraction that describes how much of the goal has been achieved. Status could also be expressed in narrative terms such as "completed," "partially completed," or "not begun."

Creating Your Own Career Plan

Begin creating your own Career Plan, using the blank form on page 111. An example of a completed plan is shown on the next page based on the career of the Marketing Manager presented in the previous chapter. The example represents how this individual may have created such a plan at the beginning or his or her career.

Marketing Manager Career Plan

	Actions/Goals/ Milestones	Task(T) Goal(G)	Deliverables	Support	Due Date	Status
1.	Learn product	T	Study product specifications	Sales Training Group	By end of training	100% complete
2.	Complete sales training	G	Complete six week course	Sales Training Group	Nov. 30th	100% complete
3.	Meet customers in assigned sales territory	T	Within 90 days of assignment to territory	Former Sales Rep	End of Feb.	100% complete
4.	Meet sales goals for territory	G	Meet sales target for first territory assigned	Supervisor, Marketing Dept, Production	End of first year on job	65% complete
5.	Exceed sales target	G	Exceed sales target for territory	Supervisor, Marketing Dept, Production	End of second year in territory	100% complete
6.	Assignment to larger territory	G	Meet company's requirement to be promoted to larger territory	Supervisor, Marketing Dept, Production Group	Within three years	100% complete
7.	Marketing Representative	G	Promote to level of Marketing Rep.	VP Sales and Marketing	Within 7 years with company	100% complete
8.	Improve company's marketing program	T	Introduce new marketing strategy for company	VP Sales and Marketing	2 years after moving into Mkt.	100% complete
9.	Marketing Manager	G	Promote to Marketing Manager.	VP Sales & Marketing; Vice-President Operations	Within 10 years with company	100 % complete
10.	MBA degree	G	Earn MBA degree	Family, co's Educ. Assist. Program	Within 10 years with co.	100% complete
11.	VP Sales & Marketing	G	Distinguished marketing performance	CEO, President of company	Within 15 years with company	50% complete
12.	Early retirement	G	Achieve financial security	Co., family, financial planner	25 years	25% complete

118

Using your Career Plan

Plans can only work if they are utilized. Your Career Plan must be a tool that you regularly update and review. Just as destinations often change from the time that a journey is begun until it is finally concluded, so do careers. It is amazing how often people end up in fields or careers very different from their academic majors or training. Your Career Plan may not always get you to your ultimate destination, but it can serve as a valuable guide to help you find your way along your journey. Show your Career Plan to your boss and other key people in your life, both professional and personal. Discuss the possibilities that you have mapped out with these people and gain a better understanding of how they feel about where you hope to be in the future. However, a word of caution: you may hear feedback from these individuals that your goals or timetables are unrealistic. Don't let anyone talk you out of goals that are important to you and that you think can be achieved. Simply tell these people that this is your plan and you're sticking to it, at least for now. Explain to them that the plan can be modified at any time, if necessary. Remember, if you can't dream it, you probably can't achieve it either.

Diversity of Assignments

Your career plan is really a learning journey that you undertake during your lifetime. Learning never ends, regardless of what stage you are in during your career. You need to seek opportunities to learn new things. Often, the more diverse your career experiences, the more effective and valuable you are in your job. Diverse job experiences teach you different skills.

119

Don't be afraid to try something new. The most valuable skill that someone can have today is the ability to learn a new job. New challenges can help you develop different skills and abilities that you never realized you possessed. Change can energize your career, providing you with a new set of challenges and goals to be achieved.

Perhaps the most valuable lesson that diversity in career assignments teaches you is that there are many ways to achieve the same results. If you have limited career experiences, you may also have limited perspectives on how to accomplish goals as well as solve problems. "If the only tool that you have is a hammer, you tend to see every problem as a nail." There is any number of ways to reach the same destination. The journey is more interesting if you don't always travel down the same roads every time.

Not in the Plan

Just like life, your career may be full of surprises along the way. You need to be somewhat prepared for the unexpected to occur during your career. Even the best laid plans of mice and men often go astray. You have to expect there to be detours along your career roads. If your plan is changed or you are put on a different career path, you need to be able to adapt to these new conditions. Don't get so entrenched in your career plan that you can't navigate another plan that you may be forced to travel. Think about how you would adapt if your plan suddenly were changed. What things would you do that would be the most adaptive to the situation? How would you still reach the ultimate goals and objectives you have for your career if your career roads were suddenly changed? Giving some thought to these contingencies and planning for them can be very beneficial should these events actually come to fruition.

Thinking About Your Career Differently

Sometimes it is helpful to *think outside the box* when it comes to your career. Looking at your career from a different perspective can give you valuable insights that you would not otherwise have ever envisioned. In the next exercise, you are asked to stretch your imagination a bit to think about your career as if it were a photograph that only you, as the camera, can create.

Career Developer Camera

Imagine that you are a camera designed exclusively to develop photographs of your career. What type of picture would you envision your career to be? What would be the setting, scene, subjects, background, focus, and perspective of this picture? Now answer the following questions:

- If you were to take a picture of your career today, what would it look like?

- How would you like this picture to look in the future?

- How long do you think it should take for this picture to develop?

- What do you need to consider and what actions should you take today to help make this picture become a reality in the future?

121

In order to help your career "picture" develop, ask yourself the following questions:

- What exposure will you need?

- What background will be necessary?

- What is your development process?

- What focus will you need?

- What equipment will be required?

- How much development time will be needed?

- What subjects need to be included?

- What image will be projected?

- What perspective will you have?

- What is your vision for your career picture?

- Are you on the way to making this vision become a reality?

Chapter Summary

Planning is important in anything you do in life and this is particularly true when it comes to your career. Without a plan or road map to follow, you will be far less likely to reach your desired destinations. Your goals and even your destinations may change, but the need to have a vision of where you are going will always be important. Plans need to be flexible and adaptable to the current conditions. There are many paths that can be taken that ultimately lead to the same destination. Don't become so entrenched in your planning that you can't adapt to alternate career roads that you may have to travel along the way. Plan ahead to reach your career goals, but be willing to change course if the situation requires a change in direction.

CHAPTER SIX

Personalities at Work

We don't always behave the same way at work as we do in our personal lives. Many times the job itself requires certain behaviors that may not always come easily or naturally to you. The Working Personality Styles Profiler is a tool designed to help you better understand both your *natural* personality style and your *learned* personality style. The Working Personality Styles Profiler will also help you to set goals as a means of learning to deal more effectively in interpersonal working situations in the future. Of course, these same skills can also be extremely useful in your personal life by helping you better understand both yourself and how others may perceive your personality style. One thing to keep in mind before you complete this or any other similar personality inventory tool is that there are no absolute right or wrong answers or styles of behavior. More important is identifying what you are most comfortable with and what works most effectively for you.

The Working Personality Styles Profiler will help you identify two important aspects of your personality at work. The first is your *natural personality style*. Factors of this style may indeed be more a function of nature than nurture. In other words, your natural personality style may be something that you were born with rather than something you acquired. Each of us, for reasons determined more by our nature and perhaps even genetics, has these certain personality characteristics that will always play a major determining role in who we are and what we become in life. Your natural personality style will probably not change very much throughout your life.

The other important aspect that the Working Personality Styles Profiler helps you identity is your *learned personality style*. This feature of your working personality is much more within your control, particularly if you choose to influence its factors. This is also where environmental factors come more into play. We can influence these learned aspects of our working personalities, but the environment in which we work also influences us. Many of a person's career goals and personal development initiatives are focused on this aspect of our working styles and personality. The Working Personality Styles Profiler is designed to help you identify and understand both of these factors, your *natural* and your *learned* personality styles.

Identifying Your Natural Working Personality Style

To help you begin to identify your natural personality style factors, envision a compass that you might use to find your direction, be it north, south, east or west. The Working Personality Styles Profiler utilizes this same concept, but with different directional settings. The Working Personality Styles Compass instead identifies the following four directions in which one's personality might follow: Collaborate, Direct, Socialize or Analyze. These four directions are illustrated below.

Personality Style Directions

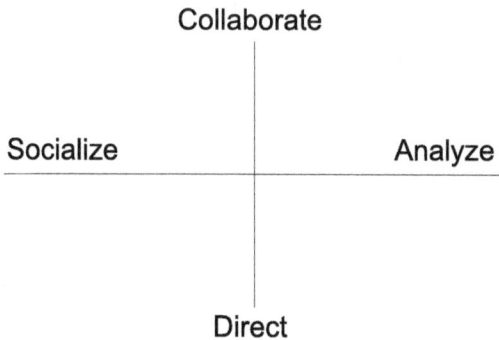

Collaborate

Socialize   Analyze

Direct

As we will see as we explore in more detail the components of the Working Personality Styles, although each of us has some aspects of all four of these directions in our personalities, there are certain dominant tendencies we naturally possess and express in all of our interactions with others.

In the following figure, you will see these personality directions presented in a matrix. This matrix is designed to show these personality directions as two continuums: Socialize-Analyze and Collaborate-Direct. On the horizontal axis is shown the personality directions of Socialize and Analyze. On the vertical axis is shown Collaborate and Direct. Each of these continuums is numbered 1 through 20. What this matrix is designed to illustrate is that each person's natural working personality style can be measured in terms of his/her tendency to either socialize or analyze and to either collaborate or direct. The following 10 questions will help you identify your natural working personality style.

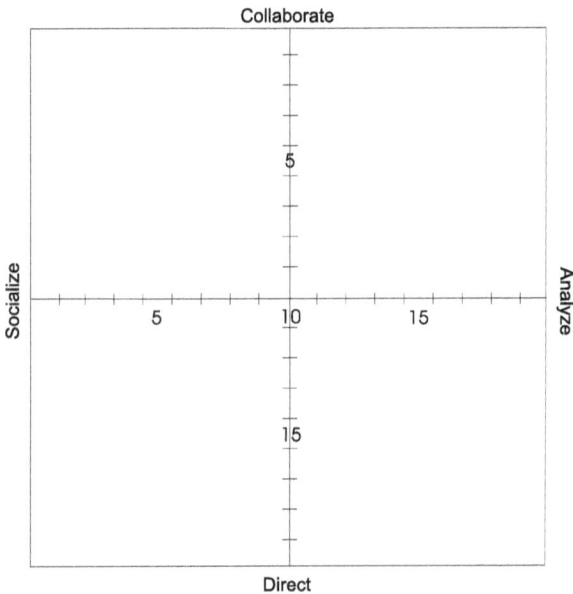

Part I: Socialize-Analyze Questions

These first 5 questions are designed to measure your basic working personality style in relation to your tendency to either socialize or analyze in situations at work. Answer each question by marking the response that most closely describes how you would likely react or respond in each of the situations presented.

1. When faced with a difficult problem at work, which of the following answers best describes how you would go about trying to find a solution?

    a. Get together with a group of coworkers to discuss the problem.

    b. Ask several coworkers their opinion of what action to take.

    c. Investigate how similar situations were corrected in the past and develop a comparable solution plan.

    d. Gather and analyze all of the data available to you in order to make the best possible decision concerning the solution to the problem.

2.   You have just discovered a problem with something
     you have been assigned to work on. What would you
     most likely do first?

     a.   Tell a coworker what you have discovered.

     b.   Tell your supervisor what you have discovered.

     c.   Investigate the problem to make sure you
          understand it before telling anyone else about it.

     d.   Start collecting data about the problem to better
          understand its cause and potential solution.

3.   You recently have heard about a job in your
     organization to which you would love to be assigned.
     What would you most likely do first?

     a.   Ask your coworkers what they think your chances
          are of getting the job.

     b.   Tell your supervisor that you are interested in the
          job.

     c.   Find out what the procedure is for applying for
          the job and begin the process.

     d.   Complete or update your resume and cover letter
          to reflect why you are qualified for the job.

4. The boss tells you that he/she wants to meet with you at the end of the day without telling you the reason. How would you react?

   a. Ask your coworkers if they have also been told the same thing by the boss.

   b. Ask your boss what the meeting is about.

   c. Review all of your recent assignments to ensure that you could answer any questions your boss might have about them.

   d. Develop a brief summary of all of your most recent assignments to bring your boss up-to-date on what you have been working on lately just in case that's what he/she wants to talk about this afternoon.

5. You have just been assigned to a new area of your organization. What might be your first objective in this new assignment?

   a. Meet or get to know better the other employee(s) in this new area of the organization.

   b. Take steps to ensure that you don't do anything to get off to a "bad start" with your new coworker(s).

   c. Find out as much as you can about the responsibilities of the new assignment.

   d. Gather all the data and written information made available to you about your new assignment and review this as soon as possible.

131

Part II: Collaborate-Direct Questions

The next 5 questions are designed to measure your basic working personality style tendency to either collaborate or direct. Again, mark the response that most closely describes how you would likely react or respond in each of the situations presented.

1. Which of the following descriptions most applies to you when working as part of a team or work group?

   a. A team player.

   b. A contributing member.

   c. An important factor in the realization of the team's or group's goals.

   d. An influential factor in the decisions of the team or group.

2. Do you feel that most problems at work are caused by:

   a. Lack of cooperation.

   b. Lack of communication.

   c. Lack of resources.

   d. Lack of leadership.

3.   Would those who work closest to you most likely describe you as:

    a.   Amiable.

    b.   Cooperative.

    c.   Motivated.

    d.   Influential.

4.   When put in a leadership role, how do you make decisions?

    a.   Allow decisions to be made by group consensus.

    b.   Give the team a great deal of input on the decision.

    c.   Consider the input of others before making a decision.

    d.   Listen to the input of others but make decisions based on what you believe is the best course of action.

5.   What qualities do you most admire in a leader?

    a.   Caring.

    b.   Understanding.

    c.   Wisdom.

    d.   Decisiveness.

Scoring

In Part I of the questionnaire, use the following key to score
your answers:

    a = 1

    b = 2

    c = 3

    d = 4

Next, add up the total score for the questions in Part I. On the
Collaborate-Direct graph, mark an X where your score would
fall along the horizontal Socialize-Analyze axis.

Repeat this same process for your answers on Part II of the
questionnaire. Mark your total Part II score along the vertical
Collaborate-Direct axis.

Note: A higher or lower score on either of these continuums
does not indicate in any way the correctness of any of your
answers. These numeric values only indicate where on the
profile your Working Personality Style should be placed.

Working Personality Styles

The next figure shows how the intersection of your score along each axis results in identifying your Working Personality Style as a Team Player, Decision Maker, Consultant or Strategist. Identify the style in which the profile results have placed you. Keep in mind that this style is based on answers you gave to the questions in Parts I and II and are reflective of how you currently perceive yourself. Others may perceive you differently, and even your self-perceptions can change over time. Also, it is important remember that each of these Working Personality Styles is very effective in both work and social situations. Again, what is most important is to understand your own style and how you can maximize your natural abilities and potential.

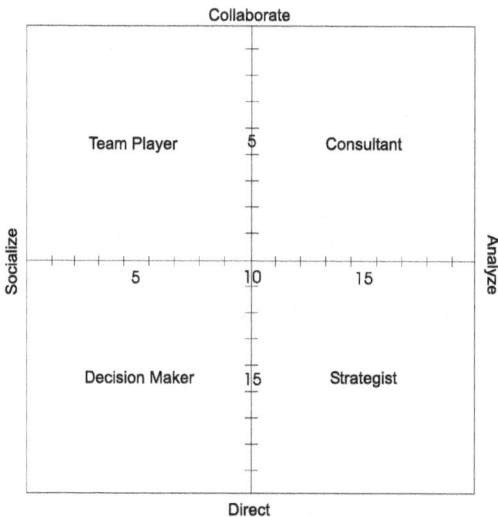

A brief description of each of these Working Personality Styles is provided below. See how closely each description matches what you perceive to be your own Working Personality Style. Keep in mind that our personalities are both complex and dynamic and can't always be summarized accurately in brief descriptions such as those provided below. Rather, these descriptions are presented to provide you with a picture of the general tendency or direction of your own unique Working Personality Style to help you better understand your strengths and potential as perceived not only by others but also by yourself.

- **Team Player.** This Working Personality Style is focused on both collaborate and socialize dimensions of the Working Personality Styles Profiler. A Team Player works especially well in groups and is dedicated to helping others on the team reach shared goals for success. This personality style tends to seek consensus among coworkers, trying to find solutions to problems that can be supported by most or the entire group. Personal relationships are important to this personality style and conflicts with coworkers tend to be avoided. Success for the Team Player is something to be shared and enjoyed with others.

- **Consultant.** This Working Personality Style scores high on both collaborate and analyze dimensions of the profiler. This style works towards group unity and problem solving by considering the input and suggestions of each member. However, the experience and expertise of each individual is considered when accepting this input. The Consultant Working Personality Style seeks to utilize the talent and ability of each person to reach group goals. Past successful group- or team-oriented solutions to problem solving are important to this personality style in developing approaches for dealing with current problems at work.

- **Decision Maker.** A Decision Maker Working Personality Style is strong in both socialize and direct personality tendencies. This personality style is often found in those in leadership positions but not exclusively. Decision Maker personalities can be found at all levels of an organization and positions, often in the role of the informal leader of the group. These are the individuals who may serve as spokespersons for the groups. Decision Makers are usually very good communicators and often very good listeners but ultimately make up their own minds on important issues. Decision Makers tend to be social in nature and develop strong relationships at work.

- **Strategist.** A Strategist Working Personality Style is focused more on analyze and direct tendencies. Working relationships are important to the strategist, but this personality style is more influenced by facts and data supporting a decision or opinion. The Strategist makes decisive decisions based on the facts. Factors that have created past successful solutions are important to the Strategist Working Personality Style in formulating future plans. Strategists may be in leadership roles or play a supporting role, providing important input and insight into the decision-making process at any level of the organization.

Learned Styles

Up to this point, the Working Personality Styles Profiler has focused on the natural aspects of one's personality. As mentioned earlier, you were probably born with these tendencies and they are unlikely to change significantly. However, there are other aspects of your working personality that you do have control over and that can be learned over time. These *learned* styles are actually the same as the *natural* styles but not as dominant. Learned styles reflect more specific behaviors rather than tendencies to behave in a certain way.

Learned Working Personality Styles are illustrated in the following figure. As shown, a Team Player Working Personality Style would have a tendency to either collaborate, analyze, direct or socialize. This helps explain the complexity and dynamics of our personalities. Often, these complexities seem to be contradictory, such as the case of a Team Player with a learned *direct* personality style, or in other words a *Direct Team Player*. This might be an individual who would tend to become the spokesperson for the team or group to which he/she might belong. Or a Strategist Personality Style may have developed a learned style of socialize even though his/her natural personality directions are more towards analyze and direct. These learned styles represent the way in which we learn to adapt to our working environments and are often essential to our success in our jobs.

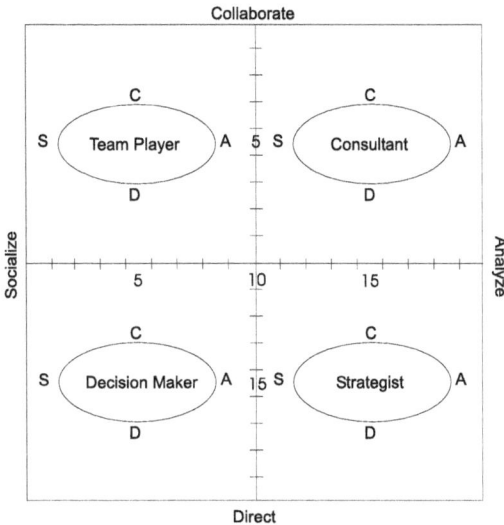

Setting Learned Style Goals

You can set your own working personality compass directions, particularly those concerning learned styles goals. In the following figure, compass goal directions for a *Direct Team Player* are shown. This Team Player's learned style goal is to become more *direct*. In other words, this individual wants to move more toward the direct traits on the Collaborate-Direct continuum. As a guide, this individual could look at the "c" and "d" responses for the questions asked on the Collaborate-Direct questionnaire. This does not mean that this individual's basic working personality will change but that some of his or her behaviors would become more direct. This could help achieve a development goal or career objective requiring a more direct style to complement his/her Team Player Working Personality Style.

Now, again utilizing your Working Personality Styles graph, set your personal learned style goals for the working personality you identified for yourself, based on your own career goals and objectives.

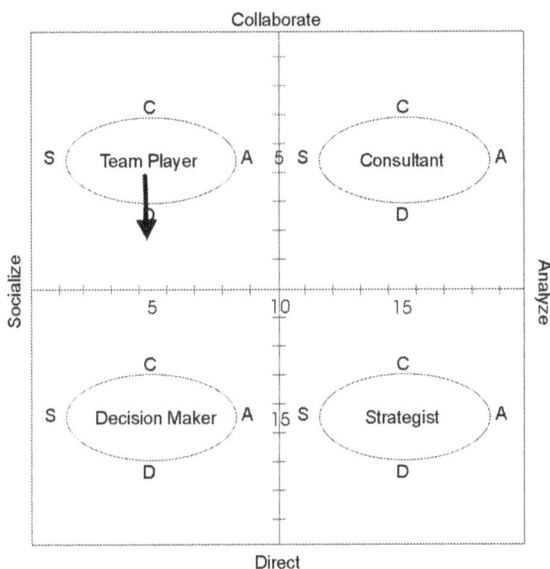

Chapter Summary

Gaining a better understanding of both your *natural* and *learned* working personality styles can help you become more effective at your job and better able to compete in the Rat Race at Work. The four styles presented in the profiler are each effective ways to deal with others in your work life as well as your personal life. It is important that you maximize both your natural and learned personality styles to establish and maintain stronger interpersonal relationships with others important to you at work and at home.

Utilize your better understanding of both your natural and learned working personality styles to help you reach all your goals in life in the future.

CHAPTER SEVEN

The Rat Pack Revisited

The infamous Rat Pack led by legendary crooners Frank Sinatra and Dean Martin, and their swinging Las Vegas nightlife style, have been immortalized in television, movies and books. Although few, if any, of us could ever even dream of leading such a lifestyle, we each form our own version of *Rat Packs* at work. These packs are a very important part of our lives. They help us deal with the many challenges that we face. These bonds provide us with essential support for one another in ways that could never be duplicated in a formal or official capacity by the organization. We need to appreciate the value of these working relationships and their importance to our career success and Winning the Race at Work.

A Place for Every Rat

Part of working together with others is sharing workspace. Maybe you have your own office and you don't need to worry about invading an officemate's working space. Or maybe your workspace resembles a cellblock in the state penitentiary or provides no more privacy than a downtown park bench. Regardless, in the Rat Race at Work most employees are assigned some kind of space that they call their workstation. Now these workstations can vary greatly in their opulence or lack thereof. If you are just starting out in your career, don't be too disappointed if the space that you have been assigned more closely resembles a hole in the wall than that plush corner office with a key to the executive washroom you always envisioned. Actually, it should come as no great surprise to you that there really isn't such a thing as getting a key to the executive washroom. There is no ceremony where these keys are presented to deserving employees who have earned the right to enter these sacred spaces. Most likely, regardless of how successful you are in your career, you will continue to use the same bathroom as the rest of the pack unless you rise to the very top of the organization. Rank still has privileges not afforded to everyone. But for the common man or woman, private bathrooms are probably not part of the deal.

Rat Space

So don't be too disappointed if you find yourself today in an office or workstation that doesn't meet your expectations. Consider it an exercise in character building. Given below are just a few workspace rules that you need to understand as you compete in the Rat Race at Work.

144

Don't Be a Pack Rat

People have many different filing and retrieval systems that they become accustomed to and proficient at working with, sometimes to the dismay of others. One common method could be called the *pile system*. People utilizing this system typically know exactly which pile to look under to find a document. As impressive as these retrievals might be, this is still not a good way to be organized. Spend some time cleaning your office. You may be amazed at what you uncover. And while you are at it, develop an alternative to the pile system. You will not only be more effective but also keep your office or workspace looking so much better.

Don't Leave Your Cheese Laying All Around

Remember that your mother doesn't come to work with you, so you need to pick up after yourself. Don't leave your cheese lying all around your workspace. Regardless of whether you have your own office or share workspace, you need to avoid leaving your work lying around everywhere. Cheese begins to smell after it is left out for too long, and papers and other work process material lying all around gets just as old and unpleasant.

Remember that the Cubicles Have Ears

Open work environments today present many new challenges concerning communications. It is impossible not to hear what others are saying when they are only a short distance away. This can be both good and bad. The good thing about it is that everyone has a better idea of what is being discussed in the workspace. This sharing of information can help you better understand what is happening in another area related to your job. But the downside is that there is little or no privacy or secrets in this environment. Be careful not to stick your nose into people's business any more than you can help it in this type of environment.

Don't Eat Other Rats' Cheese

In other words, don't take anything that belongs to your workspace mate without asking for permission. This includes office supplies that might be in open stock for anyone to take. Possession is nine-tenths of the law and this applies to office supplies and other sundries. A desk is someone's sacred space and shouldn't be invaded by neighboring factions.

Honor Thy Neighbors' Privacy

Sometimes you can't help but hear personal things about your workspace mates. You need to keep these things confidential. There are times when people need their privacy even when the working environment is not conducive to providing this solitude. You need to know when it would just happen to be a good time to get up and take a walk. Let the other person bring up the subject if he or she wants to talk about it with you. If this does occur, your role should be that of a listener, not a judge and jury.

Don't Tell Rat Tales

Most important, you need to keep all tales to yourself. Just because you happened to hear something you shouldn't have heard doesn't give you the right to spread it around, no matter how tempting this might be. Remember, the worm might turn on you someday.

Networking

The age-old adage, "It's not what you know but who you know" will always be true no matter what the time, place or circumstance. The more people you know, the better will be your ability to find your way through your career maze. Increasing your contact list can help you in many ways. It can dramatically improve both the quality and quantity of communications and information you receive. This is also information that probably will not be available through the *official* company communications system. This is the stuff that is only available through the informal communications network in an organization—or in other words, the rumor mill.

Have you ever wondered why it is that everyone loves a rumor so much? The reason is that people have an unquenchable need for information. It is just our human nature, perhaps even part of our innate survival instinct. It is conceivable that even prehistoric man was constantly trying to pick up a tip from a fellow Neanderthal if a huge beast was in the area or heading his way. With this knowledge he would know whether to grab his club to try to bring dinner home to his family or run for the safety of his cave. Fight or flight decisions are still important today and being better informed can be very beneficial in helping us arrive at the best conclusion. The best thing about rumors is that they are more timely and current than official company communications. Organizations have a tendency to wait for what seems like forever to announce information that has already been through the rumor mill and is by then considered by most employees to be like yesterday's news; that is, it's provided for everyone who doesn't do a good job of networking.

Networking is an important part of your career. Networking may be defined as building contacts and relationships throughout your organization that can potentially be mutually beneficial to everyone. Networking creates a web of contacts for you throughout the organization and even beyond. Just think about the myriad people you have come in contact with during your life. There are friends, classmates, teachers, coaches, teammates, etc. Once you began working, you became associated with peers, colleagues, bosses, and many other contacts both within and outside of your organization. All of these people can be part of your own Rat Pack. The point is that you don't have to be best friends with someone to network with that person. The problem is that often we tend to lose touch with the people we have known in our lives and aren't able to enjoy the benefits of networking with one another. Networking doesn't always have to be a direct link with someone else. It can involve reaching out to other people who you don't even know directly but through someone else. This expands the universe of contacts that you could potentially have by a huge multiple.

Network Webs

Think of your network as an intricate web consisting of all of
your contacts as well as the contacts of those you know directly.
This type of network is depicted in a simplified view below
showing the myriad contacts that can potentially exist in such a
system. In this model, the contacts that an individual knows
personally or directly are listed as *primary contacts* (P). Those
who are only known to the individual through others are listed
as *secondary contacts* (S). Contacts beyond secondary are
identified as *potential contacts* (PO).

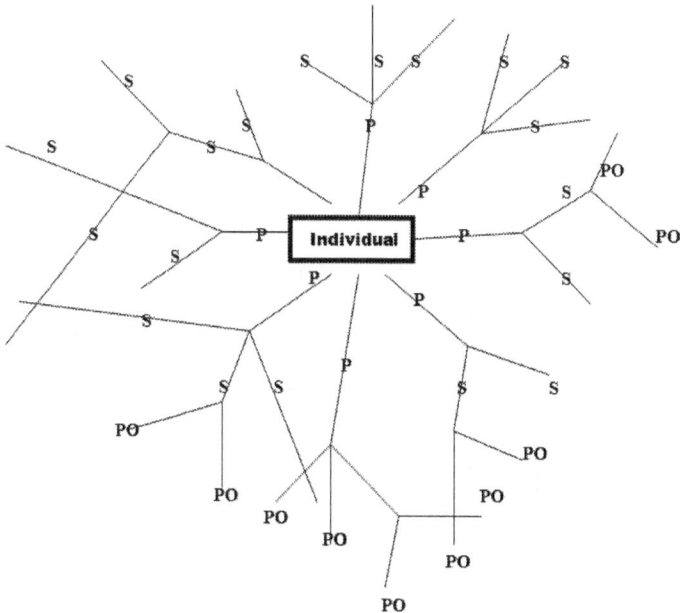

Working Your Web

Networking on your contact web is all about connections and interconnections. Mapping out your web can enable you to see more clearly the interconnectedness of these contacts. Note in the example shown above that some of these contacts intersect on the map. This indicates that secondary contacts as well as potential contacts sometimes have contact between each other. This can create even more connections for you, as these sources are part of communication webs of their own.

A popular concept today is called *degrees of separation*. This refers to the number of contacts someone has to be connected through to reach another person. In an organization, even a large one, the degree of separation to nearly everyone else is likely to be minimal.

By connecting into larger communication networks, you can tap into more effective communication networks that can continuously provide you with invaluable sources of information throughout your career. Information is the most powerful tool you can possess in an organization today and the better your sources of communication, the better you will be able to compete in the Rat Race at Work.

Connecting the Dots

As a child, did you ever play that game where you had a book with nothing but numbered dots through which you drew sequential lines in order to create a picture? It made you feel as if you were a gifted artist capable of drawing such pictures. This exercise may even have taught you how to draw on your own without the aid of the numbers to guide you. Unfortunately, your networking map doesn't come with numbers you can follow to tell you exactly the way to complete this exercise. You need to figure out the numbers for yourself, probably with little or no assistance from anyone else. The problem is that too often we forget the valuable lessons we learned growing up as children. Connecting the dots as working adults is a very important skill to learn and master. Too often we fail to see or appreciate the interconnections that exist in our lives. We don't link the many diverse aspects of our lives together in ways that would help us better comprehend these interconnections. Understanding these linkages will allow you to better understand many of the complexities that you face in your life. Connecting the "dots" in your life can help you better manage this complexity and avoid constantly repeating many mistakes. You can begin to see that there is often a common theme and connectivity to most aspects of life if you just take the time and effort to realize that they exist.

Let's look once again at the Networking Web, but this time with your own contacts in mind. An important goal in networking on your web is figuring out how to turn both secondary and potential contacts into primary contacts. A good way to begin to solve this quandary is to identify where these contacts exist in your networking web. On the next page is the Networking Web shown before. However, in this view **you** are in the center of the web. Using the web patterns shown, write in who would be your primary, secondary, and potential contacts. Add additional web connections and interconnections as necessary to begin to describe your own Networking Web.

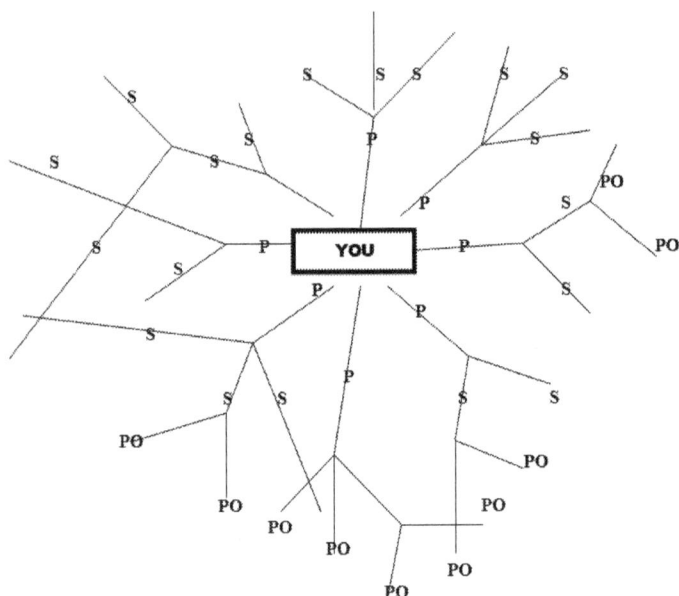

Building Rat Pack Relationships

Building Rat Pack relationships is important to you for many reasons. Working relationships create friendships that last a lifetime. These relationships can be an important part of your socialization and support systems in your life. Rat Pack relationships can also help you be more effective on your job. Everyone gets frustrated with other people at one time or another at work. Out of sheer exasperation, have you ever said, "I just wish I had a job where I didn't have to deal with other people?" The reality is that such a job probably doesn't exist. Everyone has to deal with other people in one way or another as part of his or her job. Nobody works in total isolation. So you might as well make the best of the situation. Developing better working relationships with coworkers is to everyone's potential advantage.

People working together have a natural common affiliation or bond. This bond can be one that is either mutually supportive or competitive. To a large degree, an employer will determine the approach that coworkers will take towards one another in this regard. If the organization creates a working environment that is innately designed to be competitive, it is a virtual certainty that this is the way that employees will behave towards one another. Conversely, if the organization is designed to be a collaborative environment, people will respond by working towards common goals. The problem is that organizations aren't always aware that they are creating such environments. They don't spend enough time or resources contemplating their organizational structure, reward and punishment systems and the corporate cultures that they create. And they don't take into account what employees' working personalities might be in a work environment and how their different styles could complement one another. Rather, organizations tend to have a certain perception of how employees should behave at work and punish nonconformance in adapting to this mold.

Breaking the Mold

Think about what the current organizational climate is where you work today. Do you believe that it is intended to be collaborative or competitive? An easy way to make this determination is to observe if rewards for performance are mutually exclusive. Mutually exclusive in this case means that if one person gets rewarded, the other person will not. There are a limited number of rewards available, and these are distributed by some hopefully predetermined criteria to the "winners." An even worse situation exists when these criteria are not predetermined but mysterious to the recipients and non-recipients, who therefore don't have a clue about what to do or not do to be rewarded in the future. These types of reward systems only serve to create a competitive working environment. And the higher the stakes, the more competitive everyone becomes to the point where it seems that you can't trust anyone.

To illustrate, say that you work in an environment in which there is a hand-off of duties between one group and another. In other words, one group performs a certain task or service and then another group takes over the next step in the process. Now suppose that the organization has established a reward system in which individuals or defined groups (such as production or sales or marketing, etc.) are provided rewards for their individual performances rather than for recognition of the entire process. And let's also say that this reward is mutually exclusive, meaning that only one group can receive the reward (such as a monetary bonus or an expense-paid vacation) and the others get nothing, nada, zip. How much collaboration or cooperation would you realistically expect to see between these groups in such a reward design? Obviously, cooperation would probably be non-existent. In fact, these groups that are supposed to be working together as a team might even engage in sabotage to beat the others out for this reward.

But you don't always have to play this game. You can break the corporate or organizational mold. You can recognize the inherent fallacy of such a design and suggest that the reward system be changed to allow everyone the opportunity to be rewarded for collaboration and cooperation rather than competition with one another. Unsurprisingly, such adversarial systems foster adversarial relationships. Helping to break these cycles can turn adversaries into advocates. Working towards common goals interdependently is the key to individual as well as organizational success.

Friend or Foe

No matter what goal you might endeavor to achieve, there is always going to be competition encountered along the way. This is simply a fact of life that must be accepted. In the Rat Race at Work, each person has a decision to make. You can give up and allow the competition to pass you by or you can "lace up your running shoes" and give the opposition a run for their money. The problem is that often the competition isn't so easy to identify. In this contest, they don't always wear different colored jerseys and line up on the opposite side of the playing field.

Even in the most collaborative of working environments, you still need to be aware of who may be interested in your success and who might not be your strongest supporter. Some working relationships may have nothing to do with competing for limited resources such as rewards. Often, working relationships are based on perceptions that others have about you. You may be perceived to be someone to be reckoned with or someone who can have little or no influence on the other person's career. The point is that you don't always know if someone is your friend or foe, so you need to be careful how you go. Remember, rats have big ears. What you say and to whom you say it can definitely come back to bite you. Be careful about saying negative things about others at work, particularly your boss or your boss's boss. You never know when negative things you say may come back to haunt you later. There is always somebody who will "rat" on you. It is a competitive world out there and it can be hard to always know whom to trust. Some people would turn in their own mothers to get ahead in the Rat Race at Work. Don't put yourself in a position where someone else has something that he or she can "rat" on you about.

You Have Met the Enemy

You have met the enemy and (as you might have guessed) it is you. Often, you are your own worst enemy. You do things that cause you problems despite your claims that the blame belongs to someone else. To make matters even worse, you probably repeat these same behaviors over and over again even though you never achieved any positive results with them before. It is amazing how clearly others can often see this pattern although you are totally oblivious to it. Many, if not most, of the resulting problems you inevitably experience are of your own making. You sometimes need to take an honest, introspective look inside yourself to determine what really is the root cause of the problems you are experiencing at work and even in your life. The competition, either real or perceived, may not be the real cause of your problems or concerns. You may even be the instigator of this competition. Remember, you cannot determine the actions of others. All you can do is to influence their actions by your own. Other people respond to your behavior. They give you back what you give them. It is like the traveler who, upon arriving at a new town, asked what the people who lived at this locale were like. Instead of answering his question, someone asked him what type of people he had found where he had come from on his journey and told him to expect the same at this place as well. To a very large extent, we create our own working environment by the way we treat other people.

Rats of Distinction

Having friends in high places or at least on the move upward in the organization can be very beneficial. This is where your networking skills can become very helpful. Often someone you worked with earlier in your career shoots up the corporate ladder seemingly overnight. These are people that you don't want to lose contact with just because they are at a higher level in the organization. To the contrary, these are the people that you should stay in touch with as they move forward. You don't have to ask them for anything, and perhaps it is better if you do not. Rather, you need to keep the lines of communication open with these *movers and shakers*. Creating lifelong alliances can be mutually beneficial. Each needs to stay in touch with different levels in the organization. And as they say, "It can be lonely at the top." Your former peer may welcome having a "sounding board" to bounce things off of before he or she presents an idea to the *leader of the pack*. You won't be doing your friend any favors by sugar-coating your opinions. You need to be candid but helpful if you want this relationship to continue to your mutual benefit.

Chapter Summary

Networking is important in any work situation, not only to establish connections with others in the organization but also to maintain the working relationships you have established throughout your career. You need to create a networking web of contacts consisting of those whom you know directly and these individuals' contacts and connections as well. In most work settings, there are probably only a few degrees of separation between you and the top management of the organization. Your working relationship with others in the organization plays a major role in the success you achieve during your career. However, ultimately your own behaviors, and not those of others, are the most important determinants of your success in your career and in life.

CHAPTER EIGHT

The Finish Line

Sometimes you need to redefine certain values and objectives in life. Career success can be measured in many different ways and can be very individualized and personal. At the end of your career, you may find that what you had thought was important when you first began the journey was not nearly as important in the end. The Rat Race at Work can take many different turns along the way. Reaching your career finish line can seem like an elusive goal at times, changing for many as the race proceeds

There will be many experiences that you will have along the way. Some of these experiences will be good, some not so good. Regardless, they are all part of the journey. Hopefully, someday when you look back on your career you will be able reflect about all of these experiences with a sense of accomplishment for what you achieved and with the understanding that there were many compromises you needed to make along the way.

What is most important is that you set your own goals for success in this race. You need to proceed at your own pace, not one dictated by others. Ultimately, you need to define "winning" for yourself. Attempting to achieve anyone else's definition of success would be contradictory to actual success in your career. In the end, you will be the judge of the success you achieve during your career.

The Rat Race at Work is a long process. To compete in this contest, you need to find a level of intensity that best suits yourself and your own needs. You don't want to burn out too early in your career or wait too long to make your move. Most importantly, you need to find a work/life balance that works for you and those who are important in your life. There are far too many successful careers gained at the expense of the individual's personal life. You need continually to ask yourself, "Is this a sacrifice that I am willing to make in order to be successful in my career?"

You need to make decisions concerning what cost you are willing to pay to be successful in your career. You may need to reexamine what your reasons were for trying so hard to be successful in your job. Was it for the sake of Winning the Rat Race at Work or for some other reason? Winning this race is not always the best thing that can happen to you, particularly if the reasons you entered in the first place are no longer part of your life.

And so the race goes. It is a constant battle of effort and balance. You need to have a certain amount of finesse to be really successful both professionally and personally. This is the true meaning of being a complete success in life. Don't be mistaken; winning this race will always be important. But it will be a hollow victory if the price for winning is more than you are willing to pay. This book has been designed to help you achieve a victory that is meaningful in every way in your life. You need to remember why it is that this race was so important to you in the first place.

The rest of this chapter is intended to help you define this success and decide on what terms you are willing to accept this success. The following exercises will help you better understand what this race is really all about for you and those important others in your life.

Defining Success

Remember: being successful in your career is doing something that you love to do and getting paid for it at the same time. How would you define a successful career for yourself?

At the point in your career that you find yourself in today, do you think that you are on your way to achieving this definition of success? Why or why not?

What could you do at this point in your career to ensure that you attain the success that you hope to achieve?

Work/Life Balance

Work/life balance refers to how well you deal with the challenges of both your professional and personal lives. Do you nurture one at the expense of the other?

How well would you say that you currently balance your working and professional lives?

Mark an X on the scale below where you would rate this balance in your life (ideally you would find yourself in the middle between your work and personal lives):

Work   Personal Life

_____

How would those important to you in your personal life rate how well you balance these aspects of your life? Mark an O where you believe they would evaluate your work/life balance.

If there is a difference between these ratings, in which direction does this difference point to—work or personal life?

What should you do to deal with this gap in your work/life balance?

Legacy

At the end of our careers, we want to feel that we have made a positive difference. You could call this your legacy. What would you like to be remembered for at the end of your career? Name at least three things:

1.

2.

3.

At this point in your career, do you feel that you will achieve this legacy by the time your career is completed? Why or why not?

What can you do about it?

Has your career been worth the price?

There are many sacrifices you must make to be successful in a career. You need to consider if these sacrifices are ultimately worth the price. Has the success you achieved during your career been worth whatever price or sacrifice you have had to make? Why or why not?

Have there been any sacrifices that you wished you had not made during your career?

What was the price you had to pay that made this sacrifice not worth it?

Are there any sacrifices that you wish you had made during your career? What would they have been?

What can you do during the rest of your career to make better decisions about future career sacrifices?

Rat Race Lessons Learned

What are some of the lessons that you have learned about Winning the Rat Race at Work?

How can you use these lessons to achieve your personal definition of success in the future?

What are you going to do differently in the future as a result of what you have learned about Winning the Rat Race at Work?

Imagine Your Career as a Movie

Pretend for a moment that your job is like an adventure movie, complete with all of the thrills and suspense usually found only at your local theater. This movie has an exciting plot filled with twists and turns. The characters in your story are unpredictable; some are unexpected sources of help and others are unexpected disappointments. You may need to resort to unconventional and innovative methods to obtain the information that you need to do your job. Certain actions will be risky and could threaten your security and well-being. At times you may feel as if you cannot survive all that is facing you. In the end, however, you manage to reach your objectives.

If you have ever felt this way about your job and work, you are not alone. Although work and life may not always be as exciting as an action-packed adventure movie, many similarities exist. Sometimes it is helpful to look at life and work in a different way in order to gain a better perspective on where we are and where we are going. We can view our jobs as more than just tasks; we can view work as an adventure.

A great deal of "behind the scenes" work must be completed before filming begins. An exciting script must be written that will captivate the audience's attention, a producer needs to finance the movie and a director must ensure that everything is done correctly to tell the story effectively. Stagehands must set up each scene, wardrobes need to be selected, and film and sound crews must be in place. Marketing and advertising campaigns also need to be created to promote the movie.

In the movies, studios and production companies take care of such duties. In your movie, you need to be the one to handle these responsibilities. It is up to you to produce and promote your own career. You have the most to gain or lose in your career, and you must create the excitement and direct the actions of others who are in your movie. You must decide what should be included in your story at work and what should be edited out. It is up to you to set the stage for what will happen in your career in the future. Your must be the director and the one to yell, "ACTION" to begin your movie experience.

Name That Movie

Every movie has a title, which is an important factor in its success and marketability. The title sets the tone and describes the movie, and it also gives the movie an identity apart from other movies. What title would describe the work you do and the kind of adventure that your audience will experience?

The Current Scene

Movies have scenes that show what is currently occurring in the characters' lives. What is the current scene in your movie? What is going on in your job today? Describe it as if it were a movie.

Supporting Roles

Every movie has certain roles that the characters play. Of course, you play the role of hero or heroine, but the other supporting characters also play an important part in the story's development. In your movie, what supporting roles are important in your job?

Villains

Villains do not necessarily have to be people; they can be other aspects of your job or outside sources or influences. In your movie, who are the villains or what are the factors that seem to work against you in your career? How can you neutralize the negative influences these villains exert and have "good" triumph over "bad" in your job?

Suspense

Characters in an adventure movie always experience risk and challenges; this creates the suspense and excitement of the story. At times, the viewers are uncertain as to whether or not the main characters will succeed. Often it is not until the final moments of the movie that the hero finally succeeds in defeating these negative forces. How would you describe the suspense in your job? How might the story of your job change dramatically at a moment's notice? What actions can you as the main character take to help "save the day" and create a happy ending to this movie about your job?

The Chase Scene

The chase scene is also an important element in most adventure movies. In the chase scene, the hero is either chased by or chases the villains. Often something of great value is being sought, and characters defy all obstacles to attain it. Although you may not have actual chase scenes at your job, you pursue things of value in more symbolic ways. If you do not keep up the pursuit, your goal may be forever out of reach. What would be your chase scene at your work? What are you pursuing? What or who is winning in this chase scene in this movie about your job? How could you change the result of your chase scene?

The Conclusion

Typically, a resolution of the conflict or suspense occurs as the movie draws to a close. The end of the movie sets the stage for what might happen to the characters in the future. Usually, as a result of the events in the movie, the characters' lives are changed in significant ways. Often, the characters' relationships with others are strengthened, and the characters grow closer to one another. What is the conclusion of your movie? What problem or conflict about work has been resolved at the end of your movie? How might your relationships with your coworkers be improved as a result of your movie? What new job beginnings might be created as a result of your movie?

Movie Review

Every movie is subjected to the scrutiny of the critics, who tell viewers in no uncertain terms what they think of the movie. Imagine that your job and your job performance were to be evaluated in this way. What would the critics say about them? How many stars would you give your work adventure (four stars being the highest)? What is the reason for this rating?

The Sequel

Often movies will have a sequel for further plot and character development. Will there be a sequel to your movie about your job? What would be the reason for the sequel? How can you make the sequel to your work adventure better than the original?

The Rat Race at Work Never Really Ends

The Rat Race at Work never really ends as one challenge leads to the next. It is a process, just like anything else in life. You need to look forward to each challenge that the race presents to you along the way. If you can enjoy your work and find meaning in the accomplishments that you achieve, you are far ahead in the game. Your career is just one aspect of who and what you are, and the Rat Race at Work shouldn't overpower the other facets of your life. You need to strive for that balance in life that will make you the happiest. Being successful in one part of your life doesn't necessarily make you successful in the others. Work hard, play hard and love those who are most important in your life. These are the roads that truly lead to success.

Good luck in Winning the Rat Race at Work.

About the Author

Peter R. Garber is the author of over 40 training, customer service, supervisory development, human resources, leadership and management articles and books. Mr. Garber has worked as a human resources professional for over 25 years in a variety of roles and positions. His expertise in career development and organizational change has enabled him to develop the unique concepts and principles presented in *Winning the Rat Race at Work*. His most recent books *Turbulent Change: Every Working Person's Survivial Guide* and *10 Natural Forces for Business Success* also highlight Mr. Garber's creative approach to the many challenges facing employees and managers in today's increasingly challenging workplace.

Mr. Garber received his undergraduate degree from the University of Pittsburgh and completed his graduate work at St. Bonaventure University. Mr. Garber, his wife Nancy, and daughters Lauren and Erin reside in Pittsburgh.

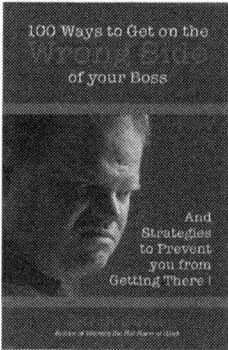

Need More Help with the Politics at Work?

100 Ways To Get On The Wrong Side Of Your Boss (And Strategies to Prevent You from Getting There!) was written for anyone who has ever been frustrated by his or her working relationship with the boss—and who hasn't ever felt this way! Bosses play a critically important role in your career success and getting on the wrong side of this important individual in your working life is not a good thing.

Each of these 100 Ways is designed to illustrate a particular problem that you may encounter when dealing with your boss and then an effective strategy to prevent this problem from occurring in the future. You will quickly learn how to deal more effectively with your boss in this fun and practical book filled with invaluable advice that can be utilized every day at work.

Written by Peter R. Garber, the author of *Winning the Rat Race at Work*, this book is a must read for anyone interested in getting ahead in his or her career. You will want to keep a copy in your top desk drawer for ready reference whenever you find yourself in a challenging predicament at work.

Available in print and electronic formats. Order from your local bookseller, Amazon.com, or directly from the publisher at **www.mmpubs.com**.

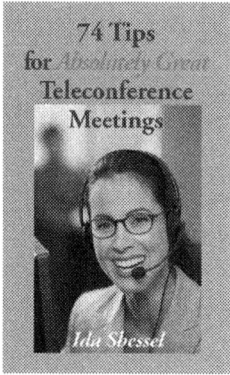
74 Tips
for *Absolutely Great*
Teleconference
Meetings

Ida Shessel

Become a meeting superstar!

With the proliferation of teleconference meetings in today's distributed team environment, many organizations now conduct most of their meetings over the telephone instead of face-to-face. There are challenges associated with trying to ensure that these meetings are productive, successful, and well-run. Learn how to get the most out of your teleconference meetings using these practical tips.

74 Tips for Absolutely Great Teleconference Meetings contains tips for both the teleconference leader and the participant — tips on how to prepare for the teleconference, start the teleconference meeting and set the tone, lead the teleconference, keep participants away from their e-mail during the call, use voice and language effectively, and draw the teleconference to a close. The book also includes a helpful checklist you can use to assess what you need to do to make your teleconference meetings more effective.

Mastering the art of holding a good meeting is one sure-fire way to get recognized as a leader by your peers and your management. Being able to hold an *absolutely great* teleconference meeting positions you as a leader who can also leverage modern technologies to improve efficiency. Develop this career-building skill by ordering this book today!

Available in electronic formats from most ebook online retailers or directly from the publisher at **www.mmpubs.com**.

Networking *for* Results

THE POWER *OF* PERSONAL CONTACT

In partnership with Michael J. Hughes, *The* Networking Guru, Multi-Media Publications Inc. has released a new series of books, ebooks, and audio books designed for business and sales professionals who want to get the most out of their networking events and help their career development.

Networking refers to the concept that each of us has a group or "network" of friends, associates and contacts as part of our on-going human activity that we can use to achieve certain objectives.

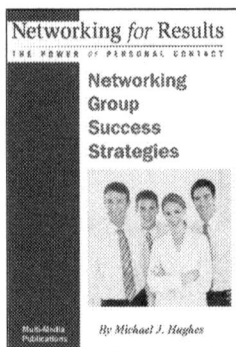

The *Networking for Results* series of products shows us how to think about networking strategically, and gives us step-by-step techniques for helping ourselves and those around us achieve our goals. By following these practices, we can greatly improve our personal networking effectiveness.

Visit **www.Networking-for-Results.com** for information on specific products in this series, to read free articles on networking skills, or to sign up for a free networking tips newsletter. Products are available from most book, ebook, and audiobook retailers, or directly from the publisher at **www.mmpubs.com.**

182

PM Audiobooks   **The Project Management Audio Library**

In a recent CEO survey, the leaders of today's largest corporations identified project management as the top skillset for tomorrow's leaders. In fact, many organizations place their top performers in project management roles to groom them for senior management positions. Project managers represent some of the busiest people around. They are the ones responsible for planning, executing, and controlling most major new business activities.

Expanding upon the successful *Project Management Essentials Library* series of print and electronic books, Multi-Media Publications has launched a new imprint called the *Project Management Audio Library*. Under this new imprint, MMP is publishing audiobooks and recorded seminars focused on professionals who manage individual projects, portfolios of projects, and strategic programmes. The series covers topics including agile project management, risk management, project closeout, interpersonal skills, and other related project management knowledge areas.

This is not going to be just the "same old stuff" on the critical path method, earned value, and resource levelling; rather, the series will have the latest tips and techniques from those who are at the cutting edge of project management research and real-world application.

www.PM-Audiobooks.com

www.ingramcontent.com/pod-product-compliance
Lightning Source LLC
Chambersburg PA
CBHW021559210326
41599CB00010B/511